THE BATTLE OF BOSWORTH
LAST CHARGE OF THE PLANTAGENETS

THE BATTLE OF BOSWORTH

LAST CHARGE OF THE PLANTAGENETS

TEXT BY
CHRISTOPHER GRAVETT

BATTLESCENE PLATES BY
GRAHAM TURNER

OSPREY
HISTORY

First published in Great Britain in 1999 by Osprey Publishing,
Elms Courts Chapel Way, Botley, Oxford OX2 9LP UK
Email: *info@ospreypublishing.com*

Also published as Campaign 66 *Bosworth 1485*
© 1999 Osprey Publishing Limited
Reprinted 2000

ISBN 1 84176 077 3

Editor: Marcus Cowper
Design: Ken Vail Graphic Design, Cambridge

Tourist information by Martin Marix Evans

Colour bird's-eye-view illustrations by Trevor Lawrence
Cartography by the Map Studio
Battlescene artwork by Graham Turner
Origination by Valhaven Ltd, Isleworth, UK
Printed in China through World Print Ltd

00 01 02   10 9 8 7 6 5 4 3 2 1

For a Catalogue of all books published by Osprey Military,
Automotive and Aviation please write to:

The Marketing Manager, Osprey Publishing Ltd., P.O. Box 140,
Wellingborough, Northants NN8 4ZA United Kingdom
Email: info@OspreyDirect.co.uk

The Marketing Manager, Osprey Direct USA, P.O. Box 130, Sterling
Heights, MI 48311-0130, United States of America
Email: info@OspreyDirectUSA.com

Visit Osprey at:
www.ospreypublishing.com

Key to military series symbols

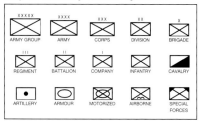

Dedication

For my Yorkist mother.

Acknowledgements

I should like to thank David Hardwick, Senior Warden at the
Bosworth Battlefield Visitor Centre and Country Park, for his help
and advice, and for literally putting the flags out for my visit!
Carolyn and Peter Hammond of the Richard III society were
unfailingly helpful in providing research material, for which I am
most grateful. Thanks also to Guy Wilson, Master of the Armouries,
for reading the text, to Graeme Rimer, Keeper of Collections at the
Royal Armouries in Leeds, for his helpful suggestions and to Philip
Abbot and Stephen Howe for providing literature and photographs.

Front cover: Details from *Prices Arthur's Book*, compiled before 1519.
(College of Arms, Vincent MS., 152 p.54)

TITLE PAGE **Early 16th-century illustrations of two standards
of Henry VII, with his badges of a dragon and a greyhound.
(College of Arms, MS. I. 2, p.26)**

PAGE 2 **Another early portrait of Richard III, painted by an
unknown artist in about 1518-23, after a lost original.
(The Royal Collection © Her Majesty the Queen)**

CONTENTS

INTRODUCTION

The battle of Bosworth is one of the most important battles in English history. It effectively put an end to the dynastic struggle known as the Wars of the Roses, and planted the Tudor house on the throne of England. Despite this significance, it is poorly documented by contemporary writers. The best known and fullest accounts were written during the reigns of the Tudor monarchs, bringing with them not only the problems of distance from the event, but also the possibility of bias and suppression of facts. Richard III has, largely thanks to Tudor writers, been blackened and deformed to suit 16th-century propaganda, culminating in the vicious, calculating murderer popularised by Shakespeare. On the other hand, and rather surprisingly, no great attempt was made by Henry Tudor to trumpet his triumph; the battle was quietly brushed to one side as he sought to hold the reins of his new kingdom. Consequently, it poses numerous problems, not least of topography, troop formations and positions. Any attempt to tell the story of Bosworth must always be tempered by this caution.

Many contemporary government papers mention the battle but provide little detail. Similarly, there is a paucity of detailed English chroniclers with useful facts to relate. John Rous, a chantry clerk from Warwick, provides some information in his *Historia Johannis Rossi Warwicensis de Regibus Anglie*, written around 1490. The other main English source is the so-called 'second continuator' of the *Crowland Abbey Chronicle*, whose record of Bosworth appears to have been written within a year of Richard's death. It may have been the work of John Russell, Bishop of Lincoln, formerly chancellor of England. Though yielding valuable details on the reactions of the nobles caught up in the affray, it says little about what happened on the battlefield. Ironically, the three best sources are continental, yet details disclosed in their writings often match fragments gleaned from English accounts. The Spanish commentator Diego de Valera prepared a memorandum for the Spanish monarchs early in 1486 and includes an account on the battle obtained from Juan de Salazar, a Spanish mercenary who actually fought on the side of King Richard. His account has been dismissed as totally garbled, but a careful reading does not support

ABOVE **Edward IV, by an unknown artist, painted in the early 16th century but based on a portrait dateable before 1472. The slightly fleshy appearance belies descriptions of this physically imposing monarch; when his tomb was opened in 1789 he measured 6 feet 3$^1/_2$ inches tall. Noted for his good looks, he was something of a womaniser. (The Royal Collection © Her Majesty the Queen)**

RIGHT **Seal of Richard as Admiral of the Fleet. He was created Admiral of England, Ireland and Aquitaine in 1462 while Duke of Gloucester. (By permission of the British Library, Seal CLI.1)**

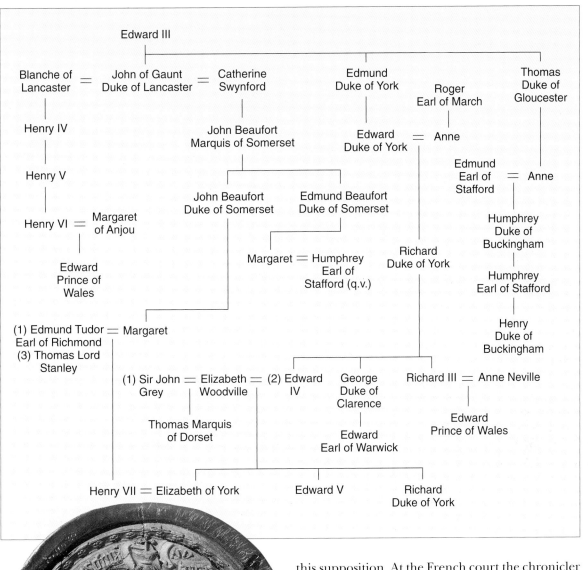

this supposition. At the French court the chronicler Philippe de Commines probably wrote of Bosworth before 1490 and, though he met Henry Tudor, gives an unbiased account of the expedition, expressing scepticism of the new king's claims. For the battle itself, a much more useful source is Jean Molinet, writing at the Burgundian court, and again an unbiased source for details probably noted down before 1490. The Scottish writer Robert Lindsay draws on oral tradition for *Pittscottie's Chronicles*, although this was written over 80 years later in the 1570s.

Tudor writers provide works of varying usefulness. Robert Fabian's *Great Chronicle*, written between 1500 and 1513, gives some information. The writer most often cited,

however, is the Italian, Polydore Vergil, who only came to England in 1502 and wrote his *Polydori Vergilii Urbinatis Anglicae Historiae Libri Vigintiseptem* between about 1503 and 1513. In true Renaissance style, he gives a careful, detailed account, presumably using information from those few veterans who were still alive. Unfortunately, many later reconstructions have been based not on Vergil's original, but rather on the translation made by Edward Hall in about 1540, which includes items such as lengthy battle speeches, added by Hall for rhetorical purposes. Lastly, there are the ballads, the earliest being *The Rose of England*, probably composed in 1485, but only surviving in a 17th-century version. *The Ballad of Bosworth Field* was probably originally composed by a member of the Stanley retinue, but again is only extant in a mid-17th-century copy, though a late 16th-century prose summary of an earlier version also survives. The third ballad, *Lady Bessy*, a story about Elizabeth of York, is a romantic late 16th-century work, but some elements may be of early 16th-century date. Despite their obvious overworking, these ballads do contain useful information, not least a list of 100 nobles and knights who were with Richard III, and which appears to be largely accurate.

England had travelled along a somewhat rocky road to reach Bosworth Field. Many soldiers had returned from the long years of intermittent strife in France known as the Hundred Years War, which closed with the expulsion of the English in 1453. Some of those men would now be recruited for the struggles for the crown of England that became known as the Wars of the Roses. The battle of Bosworth, though not the final clash (this honour fell to the battle of Stoke in 1487) was the culmination of the contest. The death of the last Yorkist king, Richard III, and the accession of Henry Tudor, set the seal on a new dynasty.

Though the battles in these wars could be bloody in the extreme, it has been recognised that there was actually little real disruption to the English countryside. Few towns or castles were attacked; indeed, many of them could not have sustained a siege of any ferocity. The campaigns themselves were short-lived; it has been estimated that the entire campaigning period for the Wars of the Roses as a whole was only twelve months.

The initial disputes between the Lancastrians and Yorkists were over bad government. At this stage there does not seem to be much evidence that King Henry VI was threatened in person. Indeed, after the first battle of St Albans in 1455 he was treated with great respect, and the Yorkist opposition professed their loyalty. However, probably because of the implacable opposition of his wife, Queen Margaret, and her noble supporters, the Yorkists had little alternative but to harden their own opposition. In 1460 Richard, Duke of York, formally laid claim to the throne. On 30 December in that same year the impetuous Richard was killed along with many Yorkist nobles at the battle of Wakefield. So ruthless was the barbaric march south by the Lancastrian forces, which included Welsh and Scots units, that Londoners recoiled at the prospect of the Lancastrian monarch. Margaret withdrew, and Richard's son, Edward, arrived instead in the capital. On 4 March 1461 he was proclaimed as Edward IV by Richard Neville, Earl of Warwick, the 'Kingmaker'.

On 29 March Edward confronted the Lancastrians at Towton, and in the bloodiest

After the Battle of Tewkesbury Edward IV had a number of Lancastrian nobles dragged from the abbey. Edmund Beaufort, Duke of Somerset, is shown here about to be beheaded after a summary trial. (Universiteitsbibliotheek, Ghent, MS. 236)

battle ever fought on English soil, the opposition was broken. Even after weeding out rebels in the north and Wales, Edward's throne was only secure temporarily, however, and in 1465 he rashly married in secret. His wife, Elizabeth Woodville, was a widow and a Lancastrian, neither of which endeared her to the king's friends. The members of her family immediately began entrenching themselves in power, and Edward himself may have used this opportunity to loosen the grip of Warwick's faction and build up his own circle. The Nevilles did not like this and Warwick found himself losing influence. He wanted a French marriage alliance between Edward and Louis XI's sister-in-law, which now seemed improbable; Louis also tempted Warwick with Holland if he removed the English king. Having made one king, the 'Kingmaker' set out to make another. He first supported Edward's restless brother George, Duke of Clarence, but then swallowed his pride and threw in his lot with Queen Margaret and the exiled Lancastrians. The result was the so-called 'readeption' of Henry VI in 1470–1, until Edward stormed back, slaughtering Lancastrian opposition at Barnet on Easter Day 1471. Warwick, no general himself, was killed. The same year, the rival houses clashed again at Tewkesbury, where Henry's son, Edward, Prince of Wales, fell. On the night that Edward IV entered London, Henry VI was murdered in the Tower. The king's brother, Richard, Duke of Gloucester, had taken the orders but there is no direct evidence that he

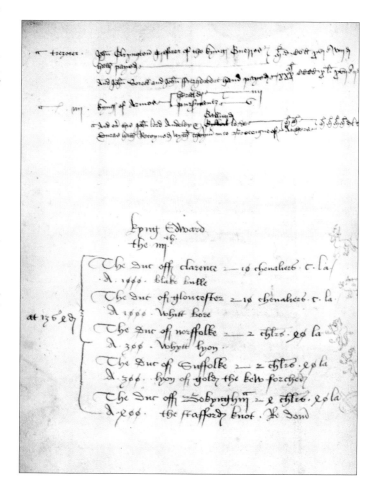

A summons of Edward IV, issued in 1475 to indent the magnates for men to fight Louis of France. Of interest are the livery badges of the nobles: the black bull of the Duke of Clarence; the white boar of Richard of Gloucester; the white lion of the Duke of Norfolk; a gold lion with forked tail of the Duke of Suffolk; and the Stafford knot of the Duke of Buckingham. (The College of Arms, MS. 2 M.16, f.16v)

was the instigator of the deed. However, Henry's queen, Margaret of Anjou, pursued the struggle against Edward. Jasper Tudor escaped from Wales and took with him his nephew, Henry, a descendant of John of Gaunt, Duke of Lancaster and the last Lancastrian male heir; in this young man lay the last hope for the Lancastrians.

At this time Richard of Gloucester was a staunch ally of his brother King Edward and was richly rewarded. Already Warden of the West Marches towards Scotland, he was made Warden of the Middle and East Marches, with control over the Earl of Northumberland. He ruled the area well and won the love and respect of the people of York. Richard was also given stewardship of all lands of the Duchy of Lancaster in the north, and lands forfeited by Lancastrian lords, including those of the Earl of Oxford.

Further clashes occurred, but Queen Margaret failed to dislodge Edward, who died on 9 April 1483, two weeks after suffering what appears to be a stroke. His son, the boy prince Edward, was now proclaimed king. If he was at York, Richard of Gloucester may

The large Norman keep in Middleham Castle, one of Richard's favourite residences. His son, Edward, was born and died in the castle.

actually have received rumours of his brother's death before it had happened, since news reached that city on 6 April. However, it gave him time to plan. For two months he behaved as befitted his position of Protector, receiving an oath of obedience from the lords and gentry of the area. There is no evidence, despite the words of Shakespeare and other later writers, of any plot to clear a path to the throne or to take the crown until the end of April. By then Richard was riding south and received reports that the Woodvilles were capitalising on their situation. At Northampton he and the Duke of Buckingham found they had missed the royal party, which had moved to Stony Stratford during its progress down Watling Street towards London. Earl Rivers (the young king's Woodville uncle) had stayed behind to greet Richard, but the following morning Rivers was arrested for treason and sent north, while Edward was taken under Richard's protection. They rode on to London to a great welcome on 4 May, while wagon loads of weapons bearing Woodville badges were paraded in the city as evidence of a plot. By the second week in June London was tense with rumour and intrigue. Richard knew that his only way to real power now was a complete take-over. On Friday 13 June, Edward IV's chamberlain, Lord Hastings, was arrested for treason during a council at the Tower of London, dragged out and beheaded on Tower Green. A number of other potential enemies were rounded up. By this time Edward's widow, Queen Elizabeth Woodville, had sensed extreme danger and had taken the rest of her family to the sanctuary of Westminster Abbey. Richard used the Archbishop of Canterbury to persuade the queen to release Edward's younger brother, Richard, Duke of York, so that the boy could keep Edward company in the Tower, a royal palace as well as a fortress and prison. The queen's relatives, Earl Rivers, Lord Grey, and Sir Thomas Vaughan were arrested on charges of plotting against the king and executed at Sheriff Hutton in Yorkshire.

On Sunday 22 June, Dr Ralph Shaw proclaimed at St Paul's Cross that the two princes were bastards. This notion had been passed to Richard of Gloucester by Robert Stillington, Bishop of Bath, who averred that Edward IV had made a marriage contract with another woman before Elizabeth Woodville. It was repeated two days later by Buckingham, who added that Edward, son of the duke of Clarence, was also ineligible to succeed as his father was a traitor. On 26 June, therefore, Richard received the petition at Baynard's Castle near Blackfriars, and rode in procession to Westminster Hall to be acclaimed as Richard III.

THE COMMANDERS

RICARDIANS

Richard III was born in October 1452, the son of Richard, Duke of York, and Cecily Neville. Created Duke of Gloucester in 1461 after the accession of his brother Edward IV, Richard proved a loyal supporter, which is more than can be said for the middle brother, George, Duke of Clarence.

At the battle of Barnet on 14 April 1471 Richard, then only 18 years old, commanded the right-hand battle. The thick fog meant that both lines were overlapped by their opponents on their left. However, Richard had to swing round and ascend a slight slope to attack the flank of Exeter's forces, only to find that the enemy had somehow turned to receive him. He nevertheless fought well enough and held his ground until the accidental attack by the Earl of Oxford on the battle of his ally, Somerset, decided the day in the Yorkists' favour. On 4 May Richard was again with his brother at the battle of Tewkesbury, this time on the left. He was ordered to pursue the demoralised Somerset, whose right wing crumbled after being caught by a hidden royal flank guard while attacking Edward's centre. Richard faced few tactical problems other than to prevent his men losing cohesion completely.

Edward was a good military leader with a flexible attitude to war. Richard, too, appears to have been one of the more reliable commanders, and it was comforting to the king to know his brother was there. He showed courage and a willingness to come to blows with the enemy personally, and could be counted on to stand firm with his men when the battle became bloody. Richard had not had a great deal of opportunity to display any latent brilliance in the field, but he seems to have possessed a competent military mind, if not perhaps of the quality of his brother the king. He no doubt discussed strategy and tactics with Edward and would have been receptive to the king's ideas. The only illuminated manuscript known to have been commissioned by him was an English translation of the well-known military treatise *De Re Militari*, by Vegetius.

Richard also shared another trait with Edward. The king was rather too trusting and willing to turn a blind eye for

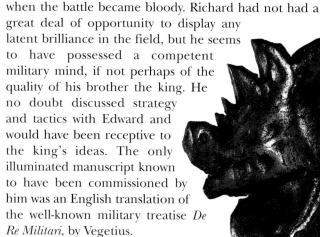

A boar hat badge, found in the moat of Middleham Castle, Yorkshire. Cast in lead, it would have belonged to one of Richard's supporters. (By permission of English Heritage)

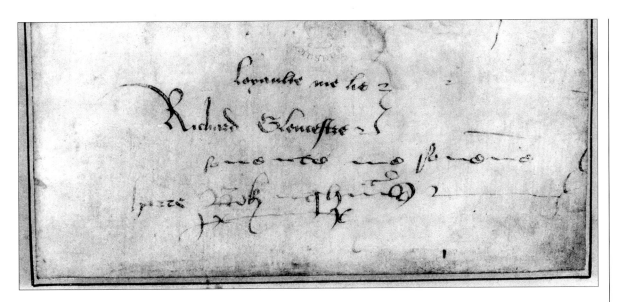

the sake of friendship. Both men on occasion chose poor advisors and allies. Whether Richard really understood the motives of some of the nobles who fought with or against him is questionable. Despite Shakespeare's depiction of Richard as a grand schemer, he does not appear to have been overly suspicious of some of the powerful men around him, such as the Earl of Northumberland, and this lack of insight was to prove disastrous at Bosworth.

It must also be remembered that, despite all his efforts to rule well, Richard failed to convince substantial numbers of people that he was worth following. Certainly the Percys did not relish the idea of a Neville as king, interfering in the north where they had been supreme for over a century until upset by the usurpation of this family. Others disapproved of the way Richard had seized the throne, which was rightfully that of Edward V, who, together with his little brother, could not be produced to silence wagging tongues. It is not the place of this book to analyse the mystery of the princes. Yet it must have some bearing on the loyalty of Richard's followers, since he appears to have been helpless to scotch the persistent rumours that the boys had been murdered. Even if someone else did the deed, Richard was to carry the burden with him to the battlefield at Bosworth.

As well as having been involved in two battles, Richard was also in charge of the campaign against the Scots between 1480 and 1483. As Lord High Admiral he had fitted out ships to counter any seaborne Scots raids. Once appointed Lieutenant-general in the North, he set about counter-raiding over the border and re-fortifying border castles. Re-appointed Lieutenant-general in 1482, he led an army of perhaps 20,000 men over the border with Alexander Albany, the rival to the Scottish throne. Berwickshire and Roxburghshire were devastated. Berwick surrendered (except the citadel) and Edinburgh was yielded after the reigning monarch, James III, was deposed by the Scottish lords. Richard returned over the border, receiving the submission of Berwick's citadel. This was, on critical analysis, little more than a large-scale border skirmish of raiding and guerrilla fighting, and does not mark Richard out as a great commander. But that is not how he appeared to contemporaries. The victor over the hated Scots, he was seen as a great military leader. 'In warfare such was his renown', comments the Italian observer Mancini, 'that any difficult or dangerous task necessary for the safety of the realm was entrusted to his direction and generalship'. In fact, Richard had fought no pitched battles at all in this campaign. Indeed, he never commanded in a battle until Bosworth itself.

John Howard, Duke of Norfolk and Marshal of England, was a powerful supporter of the king. However, his family had really only come into prominence with the marriage of his father, Robert Howard, to a daughter of Thomas Mowbray, Duke of Norfolk. John was an able soldier; he was involved in the French wars and may have been captured in the 1453 expedition. The ascendancy of the Yorkists paved the way for his family in East Anglia; in 1467 he became treasurer of the royal household and a peer, and proved a faithful servant of Edward IV, serving him well in the field as well as in council. His loyalty was transferred to Richard when he became king, and he was almost immediately created Duke of Norfolk. The new duke was of great importance. Richard gave him powerful military controls in the east, which allowed Howard to hold down this area, and to protect the approaches to London when the king was away. A list in his household accounts shows that there were a thousand men ready for royal service.

Henry Percy, Earl of Northumberland, was less trustworthy than Norfolk. From the 14th century this family had ruled the north; in a land of hard knocks they had a strong and able following, men who had proved themselves in bloody border fighting. However, the Percys had not faired well in the civil wars in 15th-century England. Henry Percy's father was slain at the battle of St Albans in 1455, when Henry was a child. The earldom of Northumberland was handed to the Nevilles instead, and it only passed to Henry Percy in 1471 after the Nevilles revolted. The new earl proved a loyal and competent soldier both in France and Scotland. Richard of Gloucester took on the Neville mantle in Yorkshire and the two men glowered at one another until a mutual agreement was hit upon in 1474. This joint supportive role in the north continued after Richard became king and it might be supposed that Percy would prove loyal; indeed, Richard granted him offices. Unfortunately in 1484 the king instigated the Council of the North, and although Percy had a leading role, he knew his ambitions were now curtailed.

Perhaps the earliest surviving portrait of Richard III, by an unknown artist, about 1515–22. He was small and slightly built but there is no sign of a deformed shoulder. (The Society of Antiquaries of London)

REBELS

Henry Tudor seemed an unlikely commander. Born in January 1457, his mother, Margaret Beaufort, was then only fourteen and his father, Edmund Tudor, was already dead. When only four years old he was taken into the household of Lord Herbert, who had assumed the earldom of Pembroke. When the Yorkists seized power in 1471 he fled to France with his uncle, Jasper Tudor. Landing in Brittany he was captured by the duke, Francis II. He then spent over ten uncertain years in which the English, French and Bretons each endeavoured to use him. Henry, despite his rank as self-styled 'Earl of Richmond', had no real military experience, unlike King Richard. According to Edward Hall's Chronicle, Richard called him a 'Welsh milksop, a man of small courage and of less experience of martial acts and feats of war … and never saw army, nor was exercised in martial affairs, by reason whereof he neither can nor is able of his own wit or experience to guide or rule an host'. This may well be pure fiction, inserted by Hall in a text based on Vergil, but despite the obvious morale-boosting rhetoric, it probably reflects Richard's view. Indeed, Henry had no great liking for heroics and his later life was devoted to methodical administrative and financial reforms, which were far more to his taste. However, he did not lack raw courage, as Richard would discover on the battlefield.

Principal among his commanders was John de Vere, Earl of Oxford. A respected soldier from the oldest surviving noble family, the thirteenth earl had made a name for himself after the Yorkists had executed his father and brother. Returned to favour by Edward IV, he then joined the invasion from France that briefly placed Henry VI back in power in 1470 (the 'readeption'). At the battle of Barnet in 1471 his leadership on the left routed the Yorkists in front of him, and although eventually forced to flee, he continued to lead raids from the coast and seized St Michael's Mount. Forced to surrender in spring 1473, he was sent to Hammes in France. Richard was rightly worried about the dangers presented by a man like Oxford across the Channel, and sent orders for him to be returned to England. His fears were justified, for Oxford indeed escaped, the orders either arriving too late or else prompting his decision to flee. He was the most important noble to join Henry's force, and boosted the prestige of his campaign enormously.

Thomas, Lord Stanley, had become controller of the royal household during the reign of Henry VI. He was descended from a family who had risen to power under his great-grandfather, a soldier of fortune in the reign of Richard II, and the Stanleys had established a power base in the north-west. Thomas's father and namesake had been created a peer in 1456. However, the family came close to eclipse in 1459 when both Yorkists and Lancastrians sought their assistance. At the battle of Blore Heath, in which knights from the area fought on both sides, Lord Stanley kept several miles back with his retinue and county levies in an echo of things to come. Indeed, he resisted the dangerous practice of openly supporting factions. His power grew and he won the love of his men, who felt they were not being sacrificed for ideals. Ironically, while holding the trust of his retainers perhaps more than any other noble, Stanley was wholly distrusted by Richard, who greatly feared him.

OPPOSING FORCES

KING RICHARD'S ARMY

Putting an army in the field was expensive. The king had to reimburse the nobles and gentry for the cost of bringing armed men to fight, which meant raising money through loans by taxing a percentage of personal wealth. For a paymaster, his retainers were his best soldiers. This 'bastard feudalism', as it has been called, meant there was always a danger from lords who could field their own private armies of retainers. Trusted nobles were sometimes granted 'livery and maintenance' for the duration of their lifetime, which allowed them to clothe their men in their own livery colours (usually the two main colours of their coat-of-arms, divided vertically, with their badge on the breast and back) and to maintain their interests. Such men were indentured, that is, a wavy line drawn through the document of agreement was cut and one half of the parchment given to the retained man as a record of their mutual agreement. Not only were such soldiers often better armed, they might even agree to fight for nothing, receiving instead the rewards of good lordship: gifts, promotion, protection or returned favours.

A number of retainers served without a formal contract. 'Extraordinary retainers' were not close to their lord, unlike some of the household retainers and 'fee'd men', the trusted supporters who would follow their master as a bodyguard, like those who rode in Richard III's last charge. Some 'well willers' had several lords. The retainer recruited men from his own household and lesser men, such as archers and billmen, from his tenantry, paid for by the lord. Nobles could thus supply large bodies of men; the Duke of Norfolk, for example, could put several thousand men in the field. They followed the long standards of their lord, decorated with his colours and badges, while a banner marked the lord in person and carried his coat-of-arms.

As well as retainers there were the common soldiers, recruited by commissions of array. Royal commissioners inspected towns and shires twice a year to check the availability of manpower between the ages of 16 and 60. The king entrusted a magnate to provide an agreed number of men for a set period, or else a magnate ordered one of

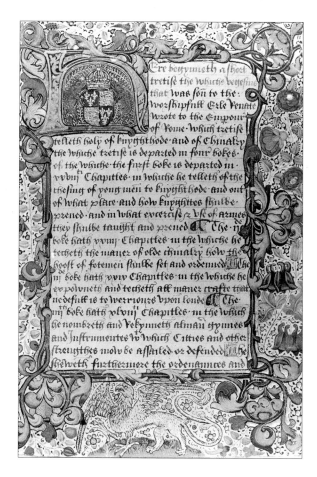

Richard's personal copy of *De Re Militari*, the standard military treatise originally written by Vegetius in the late 4th or mid-5th century. (By permission of the British Library, MS. Roy. 18 A xii f.1)

Another early portrait of Richard III, painted by an unknown artist in about 1518-23, after a lost original. (The Royal Collection © Her Majesty the Queen)

his retainers to find such men for him, from both town and shire. Since magnates and retainers often held land in the recruitment areas, it was difficult for the king to control recruitment directly, so he used sheriffs and other locals to retain loyalties. In practice, it was the magnates and their retainers who really controlled recruitment by commissions of array. If a community did not have enough equipment, then soldiers with duplicates, or those who paid scutage (money in lieu of service) had to provide it. Towns and cities were expected to pay for the muster of urban militias, summoned usually by royal letters under the signet to the mayor and corporation. Important towns on the Marches had semi-permanent garrisons, supplied by the Wardens of the Marches. Mercenaries also appeared in English armies, as well as troops sent by supportive foreign allies.

Men who were not retainers fought for wages, but this was enhanced by the prospect of loot on the battlefield. Thus any equipment received from their lord might be improved after actual combat. The result would be a very varied appearance in troop bodies, the only uniformity being in the livery colours or badges worn by a lord's man. As well as wages, a lord had to ensure that his men were fed, otherwise disaster might follow. 'Scurriers' were employed to forage for food, but stealing from the countryside would not be popular in one's own kingdom. Similarly, using a scorched earth policy to deny the enemy supplies, while sound policy in a foreign land, would be highly unpopular in England itself.

Armour

Men-at-arms comprised knights and squires of varying rank, from the highest nobles to those men who could barely afford the expense of knighthood and so had opted to remain squires. The nobles and other knights of high rank wore armour made especially for them. The best armourers worked in Germany, northern Italy and in Flanders. This meant that anyone wishing to purchase such an armour either had to arrange a special visit or else send items of clothing to enable the armourers to establish the buyer's exact size.

By the 1480s Italian and German armour had diversified sufficiently to be notably different in appearance. Italian armour was smooth and rounded in form, while the so-called German 'Gothic' style was long and slim in appearance, the armour fluted to exaggerate this rather more 'spiky' look, though the flutes strengthened the metal and also guided away weapon points. The Italian arm piece, an elbow defence and upper and lower arm defences, could be secured to the arming doublet beneath by a single pair of waxed laces, or 'points', at the shoulder, since sliding or articulating rivets, or leather straps, secured the pieces to one another. While many German armours were also constructed this way, some preferred an arm defence in three parts: upper arm, elbow and lower arm, all fastened individually to the arming doublet by points.

A number of both Italian and German armours were used by those involved in the campaigns of the Wars of the Roses. However, effigies and brasses show that many preferred a third form of armour. This was the type frequently seen in western Europe, main-ly Italianate in form, but with some German features. Plates might be slightly fluted or cusped, instead of being totally plain. The influence of the German three-part arm defence is seen in the separate couter (elbow defence), noticeable from the laced points; the couters themselves were often symmetrical, whereas Italian ones were made with the wearer's left side given far more elaborate protection. The shoulder defences, which in Italian armours could become extremely large (sometimes overlapping across the shoulder blades) tended to be smaller and often carried circular besagews to protect the armpits, as in Germany. A special type of gauntlet with laminated wrists, some with a reinforced left cuff, was different to those seen on either Italian or German harnesses. The plackart (stomach defence), which on Italian armours was attached to the upper breastplate by a strap, was riveted in place as in Germany. In England, the small plates called tassets, which hung from the laminated fauld (hip defence), were often strapped on halfway up rather than near the lower edge. The poleyns (knee defences) had heart-shaped wings which were smaller than the Italian variety. While Italian armours were usually, though not invariably, supplied with mail foot defences, the west European type was often given laminated plate sabatons as in Germany. Italian armours usually had a close-fitting helmet called an armet, which opened out at the sides in order to be placed over the head, rather like a gull-winged car. In Germany an open helmet, the sallet, derived from the basinet of the late 14th and 15th centuries, was very popular. Drawn out to a tail, it might be provided with a visor and brow reinforce. It was worn in conjunction with a bevor, a chin and throat defence secured to the breastplate by a staple and round the neck by a strap. In England the sallet was far more popular than the Italian armet, though in a higher, more rounded form than that preferred in Germany. Another helmet with limited popularity in England was the barbut, whose lower edge reached the neck and which protected the cheeks; in one form a T-shaped opening was left for the eyes, nose and mouth, and resulted in a form remarkably like a Greek Corinthian helmet. To confuse things further, foreign makers were quite willing to produce armours in the style popular in the country of export.

RIGHT **Richard III and his queen, Anne Neville, from a late 15th-century manuscript. The queen wears a heraldic mantle with her husband's arms on the left and her paternal arms on the right. (By permission of the Duke of Buccleuch and Queensberry KT)**

A contemporary portrait of Henry VII, by an unknown artist, painted about 1505. (By courtesy of the National Portrait Gallery, London)

RIGHT **John, Duke of Norfolk, from a lost window at Tendring Hall, Suffolk. He wears a heraldic tabard over his armour. Edward Hall relates that, on the eve of Bosworth, a message was written on Norfolk's gate which read: 'Jack of Norfolk be not too bold, for Dicken thy master is bought and sold'.**

It has often been said that armour was extremely cumbersome and heavy to wear, that a knight could not mount his horse without a crane, and that when flat on the ground he could not get up again. All this is Victorian nonsense; what use would a man in armour be if he could not do anything while wearing it? As a rough guide, complete armour of the later 15th century weighs 20-25 kg, the weight being spread over the body, allowing all the muscles to be used. It is less than a modern infantryman carries on his back and medieval warriors were trained from boyhood in the wearing of armour. The secret of plate armour lay in its glancing surfaces. Certain areas, such as the breast and top of the helmet, were thicker than others for obvious reasons, but the smooth surfaces, ridges and stop-ribs were designed to lead away any sharp points. Armour was made to fit so that the wearer could sit, lie down, run or mount a horse; some men boasted that they could vault into the saddle or climb a scaling ladder from the underside. The greatest drawback was that plate armour was hot to wear, and dehydration could occur. With the arming doublet in place, a harness with one-piece arm defences can be completely fitted by two attendants in five minutes. Those men who could not afford to buy their harness from a leading armourer probably went instead to a merchant armourer. Here they would find a selection from which they chose pieces to make an entire harness; the armourer would then adjust the fit to suit the buyer. Poorer knights wore older harness, perhaps handed down from father to son.

Some knights and squires wore a tabard over their armour charged with their coat-of-arms. The tabard was a loose cloth covering put on over the head, with short, loose sleeves, rather like that worn by a herald. Others might wear a long-sleeved coat similar to the civilian garment, and generally without heraldic arms. Retainers might wear a livery jacket usually vertically divided into the two main colours of their lord's arms, and with his badge.

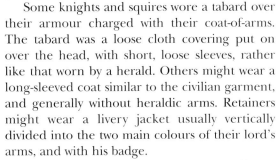

The poorer men-at-arms, and some billmen, wore proportionately less armour than the well-to-do. Some wore what was known in England as a 'splint', a form of armour which arose originally in Germany. It consisted of a breast- and backplate, and shoulder pieces to each of which was attached, by articulations working on sliding rivets, a gutter-shaped upper and lower cannon (upper and lower arm defence) both articulated to a couter. The whole was strapped round the arm and tied at the shoulder by a point. In other forms the lower cannon enclosed the forearm completely. In some cases the cuirass was worn with short mail sleeves.

For those without a solid plate cuirass, the brigandine was the most popular body armour for soldiers who could afford it. It consisted of a canvas jacket lined with small iron plates, tinned to prevent rusting. Each plate was held in place by rivets, which could be seen on the front of the jacket. The canvas was faced with a richer material, such as fustian, or by silks or velvets for wealthier clients. The rivets might be arranged in horizontal rows, or in rows with an additional rivet at one or both ends of each plate, or in trangular groups of three, a popular variety. The rivet heads were tinned, richer examples being gilded. The brigandine was usually closed across the front and over the shoulders by straps and buckles, and was often worn with a mail standard at the neck, and either a mail skirt or short pants. It might have long or short sleeves of similar construction, or else long or short mail sleeves; a few even sported plate arm-defences. Some may have been worn over a short mail coat. A number were provided with a solid plate plackart over the lower abdomen, or a complete breastplate, these being left uncovered by the fabric. It was a popular defence for all classes.

For those who could not afford a brigandine, the jack provided a surprisingly effective short defensive coat. It was made from layers of linen and was additionally stuffed with tow. The whole was kept in place by quilting, usually in vertical lines or in squares. The jack fastened down the front with laces, buttons or hidden hooks and eyes. Many were provided with a small upturned neck, echoing civilian fashion, as did the padded shoulders that were sometimes seen. A few appear to have reinforced the outer arms with chain stitched to the fabric. Some jacks were stuffed with mail or horn.

Those below the rank of man-at-arms usually wore either a broad-brimmed kettle-hat, a sallet (some with vision slits in the skull or with a visor) or a skull cap. Some sallets were very like skull-caps with a small tail. Archers usually wore a sallet or skull-cap to avoid fouling the bowstring against a brim. Many infantrymen carried a small buckler, a fist-shield either of metal or of wood with a metal boss, which hung next to the sword and was used at arm's length to parry an opponent's blows.

Horse armour was used by those of rank, the most common piece being a shaffron for the head. Complete bards, with armour for head, neck, chest, crupper and sometimes even flanks, were only for the very wealthy. Sometimes hardened leather or mail was used, or occasionally a cloth housing.

The strong countenance of Margaret Beaufort, Countess of Richmond and Derby, mother of Henry VII. This gilt-bronze effigy by Pietro Torrigiani, cast in about 1511–13, may be slightly idealised but still gives an impression of the power behind Henry VII. (By permission of the Dean and Chapter of Westminster)

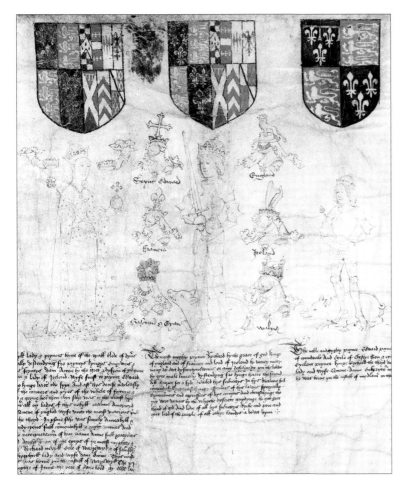

Richard III, as depicted on the contemporary *Rous Roll,* flanked by his queen, Anne Neville, and their only son, Edward. The prince's death in 1484 would shatter his parents' hope for the succession. (By permission of the British Library, MS. 48976, figs 62–64)

Weapons

There were several types of sword. A general purpose weapon, with sharp edges and a point, was made either with hollow-ground edges or else with a medial rib, making a stiff weapon capable of thrusting. Swords designed mainly for thrusting had a diamond-sectioned blade useful for bursting through the mail links protecting the joints in plate armour. These often had long grips to help balance the blade, while occasionally the front few inches of the blade might be blunt to allow a finger to be hooked over it. On the Continent it was becoming popular to add a loop for the forefinger to the front cross-guard and sometimes another to the rear. Large, double-edged hand-and-a-half swords were designed to bludgeon an opponent in armour, and were swung in both hands. The falchion was a cleaver-like weapon, point-heavy to deliver a fearsome blow. One variety of single-edged sword had a cross-guard whose front arm bent round to protect the knuckles.

Several forms of dagger might be used. Rondel daggers had a disc to guard each end of the grip and were especially popular with men-at-arms. Ballock daggers had two swellings at the base of the grip. Long knives, some almost like short swords, were carried by some common soldiers. The lance of the mounted man-at-arms swelled in front of and behind the hand and was usually fitted with a circular steel hand-guard, but light cavalry carried a simpler, straight lance.

Archers often carried a leaden mallet or 'maul' to knock in stakes or strike an opponent, and sometimes a small axe or hatchet. Most infantry who were not archers were armed with staff weapons, notably the bill, a weapon derived from the agricultural implement, with a stabbing blade, a curved cutting surface down one side and a hook useful in pulling riders from their mounts. It was mounted on a sturdy wooden haft about six feet long. The pollaxe or 'ravensbill' combined a spear point with an axe blade backed by a hammer, or hammer backed by a spike. The halberd had a large blade with rear spike, the glaive a convex blade, while the Welsh hook had a concave blade and a lateral spike growing out of the back. The ahlspiess was a square-sectioned spike mounted on a shaft. The heads of these staff weapons usually had steel strips running some way down the shaft, to prevent them being hacked off. Often a disc over the shaft protected the hand. Such weapons were designed to punch through armour or to knock it so out of shape that it ceased to function properly. Spears or even longer pikes, with plain heads, were also used.

Archers were armed with the longbow, often made of yew imported from Italy, or else of wych elm, with a string of hemp, or occasionally linen, which fitted over a horn nock at each end. No binding seems to have been used over the handgrip, nor do sights seem common. Many bows had a draw weight exceeding 45kg and could send an arrow about 300m depending on the conditions and the type of bow and arrow used. Often of aspen or ash, arrows were fletched with goose feathers. A broadhead arrow was used against horses, with cutting edges to sever blood vessels and barbs to stop it falling out. More compact heads with small barbs seem to have been general purpose types. Needle-like bodkins could punch through mail, while against plate armour long bodkins could bore a hole sufficient to disable the man inside, provided they struck squarely and did not glance off. Archers carried a sheaf of 24 arrows, either in a bag tied at both ends or through their belt, and might stick them in or on the ground for fast reloading. This increased the chances of infection from even a minor wound. Mancini, writing in 1483, notes English archers wearing tunics stuffed with tow or some other soft material, each carrying a sword and iron buckler.

Crossbows were not very popular for war in England, but were commonly used on the Continent. Some had composite bows made from horn, wood and sinew, others had a steel bow. Various mechanical aids were necessary to draw the more powerful forms, from the simple belt hook and cord and pulley for weaker forms, through the goat's-foot lever (sometimes used by mounted crossbowmen), and the ratchet with winder, to the windlass with pulleys and winders. Although these weapons were enormously powerful, a longbowman could discharge about 12 aimed arrows in the time it took some crossbowmen to shoot a single bolt. Crossbowmen were often more heavily armoured than longbowmen, and some carried a pavise, a large but light wooden shield faced with leather which could be propped in front of them to protect them during reloading. Mancini mentions that the English bowmen equalled French crossbowmen in range.

The handgun was now an established weapon, although it was still quite crude. Though triggers which lowered a slow-match on to the powder in the touch-hole were making an appearance, many handgunners simply held the match or a hot wire in their fingers. The forged iron, or

A late 15th-century south German composite armour. The horse armour was made at Augsburg in about 1480 for the Duke of Anhalt-Zerbst. Only the very rich could purchase such protection, and complete horse armour was a luxury few could afford. Though such 'Gothic' harnesses were seen in England, many would have used English or Flemish-made armour. (By courtesy of the Trustees of the Armouries)

RIGHT This north Italian armour dates from about 1450. The plates are less fluted and more rounded than the form that would become popular in Germany. Its original armet has been replaced by a barbut, and the left gauntlet is restored. The tassets, which hung from the skirt, the culet over the buttocks and the wearer's right elbow reinforce are missing. Note that the feet are covered in mail. (Glasgow Museums: Art Gallery & Museum, Kelvingrove)

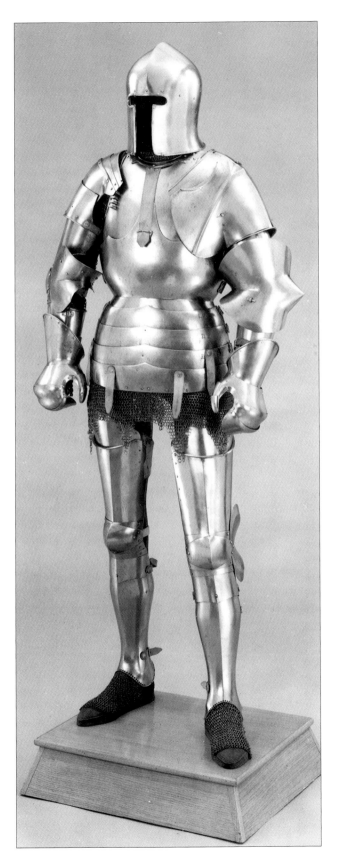

copper-alloy, barrel might be strapped into a wooden stock, or was made with a socket at the rear for the stock, or even with a metal extension instead. Richard purchased a number of these hackbuts.

Artillery was a common feature of battles and sieges by the mid-15th century. In 1484 Richard was purchasing guns and employing experts, some from Flanders, to produce more pieces in the Tower of London. Though *The Ballad of Bosworth Field* speaks of bombards, it seems unlikely that these large and cumbersome siege guns would have been used. It also mentions smaller serpentines, and it is much more likely that field guns on wheeled carriages were present. Pulled by horses and with ammunition and tools carried in carts, such guns could easily keep up with a marching army. Corned powder, which did not separate out into its component parts so readily as serpentine, was too powerful for many guns except the forged handguns and a few brass cannon. Most cannonballs were made of shaped stone, though a few might be of forged iron.

THE ARMY OF HENRY TUDOR

The rebel army could not be raised by taxing the population. Henry and his lords had to rely on their own funds or on gifts from well-wishers in order to finance the raising of troops, hence the small number involved. It should not be forgotten that 3,000–4,000 men were supplied by the French King, about 1,500 of whom were soldiers discharged from the military base at Pont de l'Arche, paid for by the King and placed under Philibert de Chandée. 300–500 were English exiles. There were also Welsh and Scottish contingents, as well as some Breton mercenaries. However, by the time it reached Bosworth the army had been together for several weeks, sharing hardship and a common fate if defeated. The dress and equipment of Henry's force was similar in most respects to that of his opponent. There may have been more crossbowmen in his ranks, however, and the Welsh may have provided many of the longbowmen.

REBELLION

In 1483 King Richard knew that Henry Tudor was waiting on the other side of the Channel. However, he was not unduly worried. His coronation had gone well, indeed, it had been attended by a heartening number of important men in the realm: the dukes of Norfolk and Buckingham, the earls of Northumberland, Kent and Lincoln and Lord Stanley. Even the latter's wife, Margaret, Countess of Richmond and mother of Henry Tudor, was present in the retinue of Queen Anne.

However, the plight of the two young princes, one of whom many considered the rightful king, must have played on numerous minds. The Italian commentator Dominic Mancini left London in early July 1483 and noted that, even then, many thought them already dead. Edward himself seems in some respects to have been quite mature and apparently expected to be killed as this was the nature of medieval realpolitik. Nobody now can say with certainty what happened to the boys. Several people have been blamed for the murder, including Henry Tudor, who would certainly not have welcomed another legitimate king after his own succession. However, it has never been explained why Richard did not simply produce the princes to scotch the rumours; nor did he deny them. Another suspect, one suggested by the earliest contemporary English record to survive, is Buckingham. He was close to the king and after Richard's departure on a progress round his kingdom the duke was left in control of the capital. A month later he was involved in a huge row with Richard, the reasons for which are unknown. Buckingham may have committed the deed without orders, expecting royal gratitude. It is also possible that he was angling for the throne himself.

The disappearance of the two boys was to haunt Richard. Initially, however, all seemed well enough. After the coronation, he progressed to Windsor and thence to Oxford, Gloucester, Worcester, Warwick, Leicester and Nottingham. He moved into Yorkshire and his own son, Edward, was created Prince of Wales at York. On 11 October,

RIGHT **The effigy of Sir William Harcourt (died 1482) in Aston Church shows armour in the style popular in England. The circular besagew at the armpit, equal-sized couters (elbow-pieces) laced on, the form of gauntlets, the tassets worn halfway up the fauld (skirt), and small wings on the poleyns (knee-pieces) are all features of such armour. Note the upstanding mail collar at the neck.**

A sallet of about 1460, perhaps of English manufacture. (Herbert Art Gallery and Museum, Coventry)

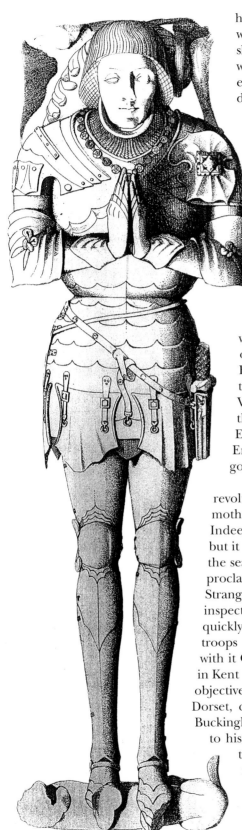

however, while at Lincoln during his journey back south, he was informed that revolt had broken out in several southern shires. What made it more bitter was that one of the main leaders was Buckingham. It is certainly possible that the duke had an eye to the throne. His unquartered coat-of-arms reflected his descent from Thomas of Woodstock, youngest son of Edward III. His father had been killed fighting for Henry VI at the battle of St Albans in 1455 and his grandfather at Northampton five years later, so he had no reason to love the Yorkist regime. As he had used Richard to help eliminate Edward's immediate line, now he could use Henry to remove Richard. It is also possible that he was simply sucked in by events and was shrewd enough to realise that, should the revolt succeed, he needed to be on the winning side. The rebellion also involved many other men of note, all whipped up by the Woodville faction and the Marquis of Dorset. In the west country, for example, the old Lancastrian Sir Edward Courtenay claimed the earldom of Devon, but here, as well as in south-central and south-east England, the chief rebels were leading men in the community, those who had been sheriffs of the southern counties and knights or squires of the body to Edward IV. It was a potentially dangerous situation, fuelled by the rumours of murder. To add to Richard's troubles, Henry VI's widow, Margaret of Anjou, and her supporters proposed the marriage of Henry Tudor with Edward IV's daughter, Elizabeth of York. The rebels had called on Henry to cross to England and be crowned king. In response, the Breton government found ships for him and he set sail, hopes high.

Another problem for Richard was the extent to which the revolt might spread. One of the troublemakers was Henry Tudor's mother, Margaret, wife of the powerful magnate Lord Stanley. Indeed, Stanley's son, Lord Strange, raised a huge force of retainers but it was not clear where his loyalties lay. Richard acted swiftly, like the seasoned campaigner he was. He moved down to Leicester and proclaimed a general muster of troops. Fortunately for him, Lord Strange threw in his lot with the king. By chance, Norfolk was inspecting his newly acquired estates in Surrey and Sussex, and quickly moved to seize the Gravesend crossings, while he ordered troops to London to prevent the rebels from taking the capital and with it Queen Elizabeth Woodville and the princesses. The rebellion in Kent broke out ten days prematurely and failed to secure any major objectives. As for the threat from the west, Thomas Grey, Marquis of Dorset, could not guarantee any safe landfalls for the exiles, while Buckingham had real problems in bringing enough of his own retainers to his standard. Meanwhile, Humphrey Stafford of Grafton seized the bridges over the Severn and neatly bottled up the western rebels. Faced by the large royal forces now speedily moving south on forced marches, the revolt petered out. Buckingham was betrayed by one of his own servants and brought in chains to Salisbury, where he was beheaded on All Souls day. On reaching the south coast Richard turned west and soon

THE PROGRESS OF RICHARD III AND THE REBELLION OF 1483

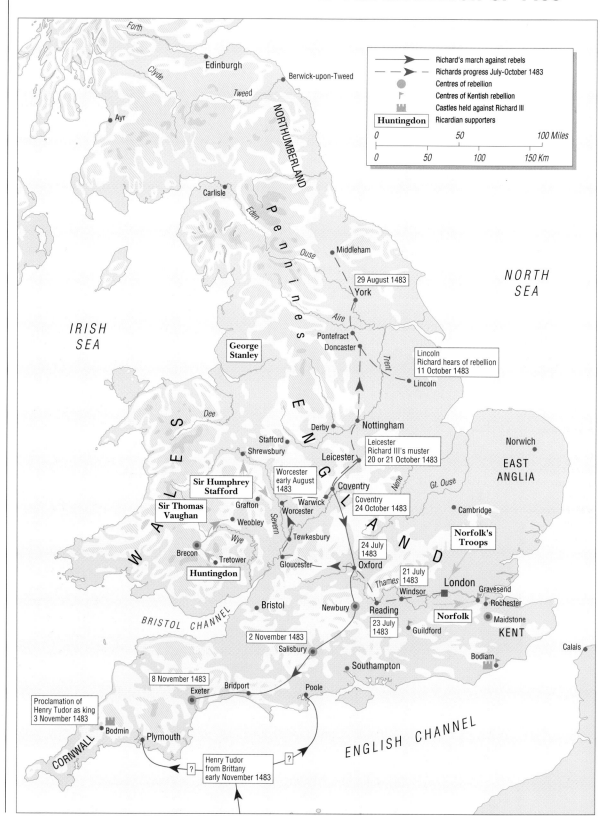

Legend:
- Richard's march against rebels
- Richards progress July-October 1483
- Centres of rebellion
- Centres of Kentish rebellion
- Castles held against Richard III
- **Huntingdon** Ricardian supporters

0   50   100 Miles

0   50   100   150 Km

Forth
Edinburgh
Clyde
Berwick-upon-Tweed
Tweed
Ayr

NORTHUMBERLAND

NORTH SEA

Carlisle
Eden
Pennines
Ouse
Middleham

29 August 1483
York

IRISH SEA

Aire
Pontefract
Doncaster

George Stanley

Trent

Lincoln
Richard hears of rebellion
11 October 1483
Lincoln

Dee

ENGLAND

Derby
Nottingham

Norwich

Stafford
Shrewsbury
Leicester

Leicester
Richard III's muster
20 or 21 October 1483

EAST ANGLIA

Sir Humphrey Stafford

Worcester
early August 1483

Coventry

Nene
Gt. Ouse

Sir Thomas Vaughan

Grafton
Warwick
Worcester

Coventry
24 October 1483

Cambridge

Weobley

Severn

Wye
Tewkesbury

24 July 1483

Norfolk's Troops

Brecon
Tretower

Gloucester
Oxford

21 July 1483

London
Gravesend

Huntingdon

Windsor

Thames

Rochester

WALES

Bristol

Newbury

Reading

Norfolk

Maidstone

BRISTOL CHANNEL

23 July 1483

Guildford

KENT

Calais

2 November 1483

Salisbury

Bodiam

Southampton

8 November 1483

Exeter
Bridport

Poole

Proclamation of
Henry Tudor as king
3 November 1483

Bodmin
Plymouth

CORNWALL

ENGLISH CHANNEL

Henry Tudor
from Brittany
early November 1483

26

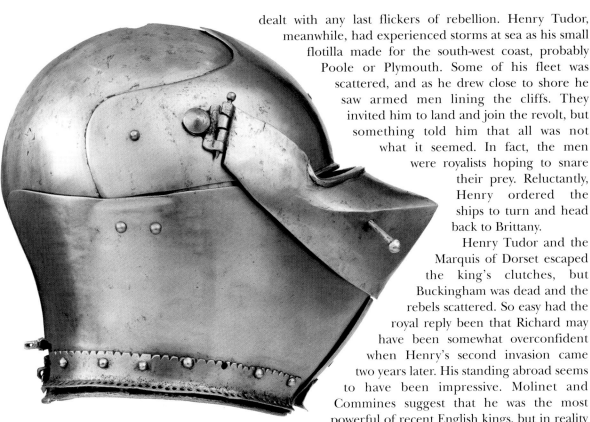

A north Italian armet of about 1450. The cheek-pieces open out to allow it to be put on and, when fastened, the visor sits over the upper edge. The staples around the brim are for the attachment of a small mail curtain or aventail. (By courtesy of the Trustees of the Armouries)

dealt with any last flickers of rebellion. Henry Tudor, meanwhile, had experienced storms at sea as his small flotilla made for the south-west coast, probably Poole or Plymouth. Some of his fleet was scattered, and as he drew close to shore he saw armed men lining the cliffs. They invited him to land and join the revolt, but something told him that all was not what it seemed. In fact, the men were royalists hoping to snare their prey. Reluctantly, Henry ordered the ships to turn and head back to Brittany.

Henry Tudor and the Marquis of Dorset escaped the king's clutches, but Buckingham was dead and the rebels scattered. So easy had the royal reply been that Richard may have been somewhat overconfident when Henry's second invasion came two years later. His standing abroad seems to have been impressive. Molinet and Commines suggest that he was the most powerful of recent English kings, but in reality the situation remained very unpredictable. No one could be sure how many gentlemen and local lords, who often led the men of the commissions of array, would stand with Richard when required. Large numbers of knights and squires in the southern shires had now renounced their loyalties to Richard, loyalties which they had given to the Yorkist kings for a generation. Many new exiles fled abroad to swell the numbers surrounding Henry in Brittany, where they were more focused, unified in one location instead of being scattered over large areas of England.

Much of Buckingham's landed wealth was given to the Stanleys, though Richard no doubt disliked their penchant for playing a waiting game at times of crisis. Northern friends also did well from forfeited estates. A number of them became southern landlords, but this military settlement was highly unpopular in the south. Richard was bestowing estates without legal assent, in what was probably a deliberate insult to the southern magnates. Much of this dealing was done while on campaign, however, and Richard was very lenient to obvious traitors, suggesting that he was being dictated to on the one hand by his powerful followers, and on the other by political desperation.

The short time Richard had as king shows him to have had the makings of a notable monarch, though opponents would say that much of his work was done to ingratiate himself with his subjects. This is too simple a retort. It is known from his personal books and prayers that he was a religious man, and in this respect contrasted greatly with his more debauched elder brother. He set about reforming morals both at court and in public, and chose ecclesiastical appointments wisely, something that, given time, may have won him the Church's support for his regime. Moreover he was noted for his generous patronage to the Church. Von Poppelau, who visited the court at Middleham in 1484, recounted that Richard earnestly wished to crusade against the Turks, who had taken Constantinople in 1453. He heard pleas from ordinary folk, corrected legal wrongs and took such an interest in the law that his work was given the nod of respect after his death. He granted land, title and wealth to friends, and forgave enemies. He refused grants from towns that he visited and, notably, abolished benevolences – 'gifts' forced from nobles by the monarch. His strong attachments in the north were also extended into the Midlands and eastern England.

At first, therefore, it might have seemed that Richard would manage to secure himself on the throne. Queen Elizabeth Woodville gave up her resistance and made peace with him. His negotiations with the French and Breton courts nearly resulted at one point in the ensnarement and capture of Henry Tudor. Yet by the spring of 1484 things were looking more uncertain. It became necessary to repeat his legitimacy to the kingship, already given in parliament, in the city halls and county towns of England. One hundred attainders were drawn up against rebels in one session, compared to 140 for the whole of his brother's reign. Then, in April 1484 came perhaps the cruellest blow of all: his son, Edward of Middleham, Prince of Wales, died suddenly. Both parents were reported as distraught with grief, not least

A Milanese kettle hat of about 1480. Though named after the word for a cooking pot, the brim was effective in deflecting weapons or missiles while still allowing air to the face. It was a popular helmet with infantry. (By courtesy of the Trustees of the Armouries)

The lining of a late 15th-century brigandine, showing the small plates that were riveted inside the canvas body. (By courtesy of the Trustees of the Armouries)

A late 15th-century infantryman. He wears a brigandine, lined with small plates whose rivet heads are visible on the surface. It is covered in red velvet and fastens down the front. The mail sleeves give partial protection. The barbut was popular, especially with archers as there was no brim over the face to snag the bowstring. The Italian bill could be used to slash or stab, whilst the hook could drag a rider from his horse. (By courtesy of the Trustees of the Armouries)

perhaps because it removed the only legitimate successor to Richard's crown. Later in the year other schemes were uncovered, some hatched by men who had been pardoned for the earlier rebellion. William Collingbourne wrote a cutting doggerel: 'The rat, the cat and Lovell the dog, rule all England under the hog'. It took a swipe at three chief councillors, Sir Richard Radcliffe, William Catesby and Viscount Lovell, the hog was a reference to Richard's badge of the white boar. Collingbourne was executed for treasonable communication with Henry. Meanwhile, increasingly short of money, Richard demanded sureties for offenders and raised loans from followers.

More rumours spread. It was said that the king, now without an heir, wished to put away Anne Neville and marry his own niece, Elizabeth of York. Not surprisingly, when Anne died early the following year it was said that the king had poisoned her. Richard went through the shaming display of denying on oath that he had any designs on Elizabeth. It seems to have done little good; even in his northern heartlands rumours were now circulating, and the death of the queen may have strained relations with the Nevilles, some of whom may have suspected murder. Moreover, the Midlands, though home to a number of supporters, also included too many lords of uncertain loyalty, while the civil wars had resulted in a lack of major magnates to provide some stability.

Richard may by now have felt that he was a marked man, but set about making preparations for Henry Tudor's expected invasion. Sir Robert Brackenbury had charge of a large force in the Tower of London. The Duke of Norfolk, Richard's closest ally, was told to have troops ready at his castle at Framlingham, to block the eastern approaches to London. Viscount Lovell went down to Southampton to oversee preparations for the naval defence of the south coast. It was said, by prophesy or report, that the pretender would try to land at Milford and so a special watch must have been kept on Milford-on-Sea in Hampshire. Similarly, the Earl of Huntingdon, Richard's son-in-law, and the earl's brother, Walter Herbert, must have been aware of Milford Haven in Pembrokeshire. The Herberts were the most powerful family in this part of Wales, but the king had also taken care to make alliances with local men. Rhys ap Thomas was paid handsomely in return for raising Welsh troops, and Richard Williams was given control of the castles at Pembroke, Manorbier, Cilgerran and Tenby. Beacons were prepared so that an invasion could be flashed by signal fires across Wales and England. Even the suspect Lord Stanley was granted permission to return north-west to his seat at Lathom in Lancashire to prepare his troops. Richard had tried to revive or expand the posting system set up in 1482, in which riders were set along the main routes, but it was so expensive that it seems to have been much reduced or terminated by 1485. Cash shortages may have also affected his use of spies in France, though he could still get information via English-held Calais. On Ascension Day Richard set off for Windsor, thence to Kenilworth for Whitsuntide, and reached Nottingham Castle, which he called his 'Castle of Care', in early June. A favourite residence, it was also well placed to allow swift movement in many directions, not least to Leicester, a day's march south, a town which could be reached by his East Anglian allies and those further north. Within its walls on the craggy prominence Richard waited for the final confrontation with his enemies, which must come soon.

THE INVASION

On Christmas day 1483, at Rennes cathedral and before numerous exiled lords, Henry Tudor laid claim to the English crown and swore to marry Edward IV's daughter Elizabeth of York. His court had grown slowly from the several hundred or so who followed him over the sea, and had been swelled by refugees following the collapse of the rebellion in November of that year.

The attempted invasion had obviously caused ill will between England and Brittany and it was not until June the following year that Richard again began probing for the hand-over of Henry Tudor. Among the negotiations was an agreement on 26 June 1484 for Richard to provide 1,000 archers, and presumably at about this time he persuaded the Breton chancellor, Pierre Landois, to hand over Henry. Landois, nominally in control during a period when Duke Francis was incapacitated, was unpopular and probably hoped to strengthen his position; Brittany also welcomed English support against the pretensions of the French crown towards the duchy. Luckily John Morton, Henry's agent, found out about the plot and sent warning, allowing him to escape over the border in the nick of time. He fled to the court of the French king Charles VIII, successor to Louis XI, who had died in the same year as Edward IV. When Duke Francis recovered, he was angry at what had happened and allowed other Englishmen of Henry's party to join him. For his part, Charles was in no hurry to assist an invasion; it suited him to know that the pretender was a worry to his English opposite number. Any overt support might encourage English assistance to Brittany, but a successful invasion by the inexperienced and impoverished Henry did not look likely. Such reticence dependent upon political realities must have frustrated Henry, but he was better placed than he had been in

Two handguns of about 1500, the upper of iron, the lower of copper-alloy with reconstructed stock. These primitive pieces were fired either by a slow match (hemp cord soaked in saltpetre and spirits of wine) or by a hot wire, which was pressed against the priming powder at the touch-hole. The ballads speak of harquebusiers in both armies. (By courtesy of the Trustees of the Armouries)

THE INVASION OF HENRY TUDOR, 1485

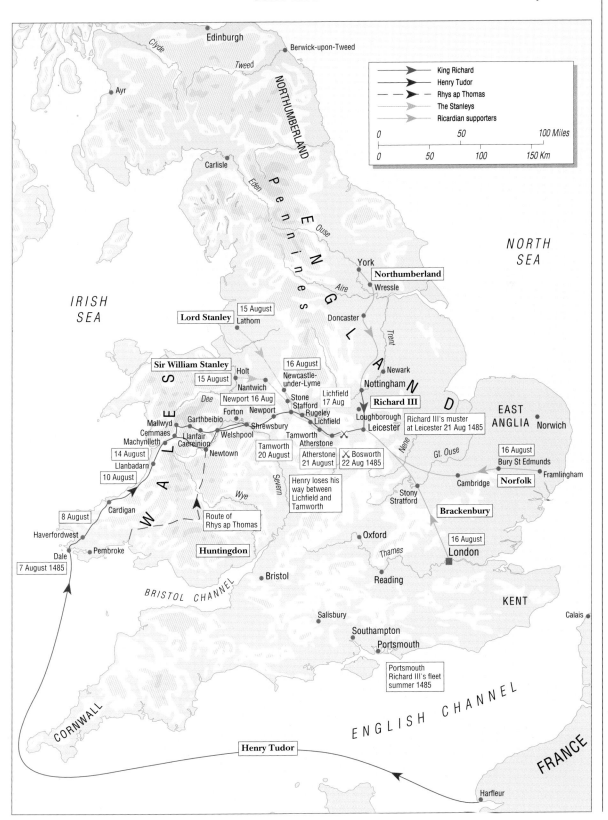

Legend:
- King Richard
- Henry Tudor
- Rhys ap Thomas
- The Stanleys
- Ricardian supporters

0   50   100 Miles
0   50   100   150 Km

Edinburgh

Clyde

Tweed

Berwick-upon-Tweed

Ayr

NORTHUMBERLAND

Carlisle

Eden

P e n n i n e s

Ouse

York

Northumberland

Wressle

NORTH SEA

IRISH SEA

Aire

E N G L A N D

Doncaster

Trent

Newark

Nottingham

Richard III

15 August
Lathom
Lord Stanley

Sir William Stanley
15 August
Holt

Nantwich

16 August
Newcastle-under-Lyme

Dee

Newport 16 Aug

Forton

Stone
Stafford
Rugeley
Lichfield

Lichfield
17 Aug

Loughborough
Leicester

Richard III's muster
at Leicester 21 Aug 1485

EAST ANGLIA

Norwich

Mallwyd
Cemmaes
Machynlleth

Garthbeibio

Llanfair
Caereinion

Welshpool

Shrewsbury

Newport

W A L E S

Newtown

Tamworth
20 August

Tamworth
Atherstone

Atherstone
21 August

✗ Bosworth
22 Aug 1485

Nene

Gt. Ouse

16 August
Bury St Edmunds

Norfolk

Framlingham

14 August
Llanbadarn

10 August

Wye

Severn

Henry loses his
way between
Lichfield and
Tamworth

Cambridge

Stony
Stratford

Brackenbury

Cardigan

8 August

Route of
Rhys ap Thomas

Huntingdon

Oxford

Thames

16 August
London

Haverfordwest

Dale
Pembroke

7 August 1485

Bristol

BRISTOL CHANNEL

Reading

KENT

Calais

Salisbury

Southampton
Portsmouth

Portsmouth
Richard III's fleet
summer 1485

CORNWALL

Henry Tudor

E N G L I S H   C H A N N E L

FRANCE

Harfleur

31

Brittany. He was now recognised as the rightful heir to the English throne, he could communicate more freely with supporters across the Channel, and he was able to receive money and men. English soldiers defected from the garrisons in the march of Calais, the most notable being James Blount, lieutenant of Hammes Castle, Sir John Fortescue, the gentleman porter of Calais, and with them their former prisoner, John de Vere, 13th Earl of Oxford. The arrival of the Earl of Oxford filled Henry with delight, for here was a diehard Lancastrian in whom he could entrust his thoughts and who would attract other recruits. Other men joined the pretender, such as Sir Richard Edgecombe, John Risley and William Brandon, who would carry his standard at Bosworth. Thomas Savage, nephew of Lord Stanley and from the stock of Cheshire magnates, was a civil lawyer in the service of Margaret Beaufort. Some English merchants played their part, supplying men and material; one such was the London draper William Bret, who bought armour for the exiles.

In November the French council, possibly fearing an English invasion and intrigue with Brittany and Burgundy, voted Henry 3,000 livres. However, the prospect of success still seemed remote as 1484 ended and the new year began. Richard remained in overall control while Henry, though stronger, was nowhere near strong enough. He was able to give a show of power when Oxford and others forced English troops sent by Richard to raise the siege of Hammes and allow the garrison to leave unharmed. At one point Richard used Queen Elizabeth Woodville to lure the Marquis of Dorset back; having made off towards Flanders he was intercepted and persuaded to return by Humphrey Cheney. Such an episode was serious, since the marquis knew a great deal about Henry's intentions; it must have forced Henry to firm up his plans for invasion before anything similar happened. As sureties he left behind the untrustworthy Marquis of Dorset, together with John Bourchier, and set off northwards for Rouen, capital of Normandy. While busy with ships at the mouth of the Seine, Henry finally heard (perhaps not until early summer) the rumour that Richard proposed to marry Elizabeth of York, Henry's intended bride, and to marry her sister Cecily to a man of no substance. This, says Polydore Vergil, 'pinched him by the very stomach'. If it ever became a reality his main prop, the unification of the houses of Lancaster and York and a secure peace, would fall away and so would his supporters. The Herberts were now the most powerful family in south Wales. Henry had fostered relations with Walter Herbert, the son of his former guardian, and tried to suggest a marriage with his sister. He also sent messengers north to Henry Percy, Earl of Northumberland, who had married Walter's other sister, Maud. Luckily for Henry Tudor, the messengers failed to get through.

On 21 June Richard issued a proclamation stating that the former earls of Oxford and Pembroke and other traitors had gone over to the rebels in France and had chosen Henry Tudor to lead them. Henry had, through 'his ambitious and insatiable covetousness' assumed the royal title. The proclamation was similar to one the king had issued in December. Next day Richard began the mobilisation of the kingdom.

The nobility and captains were ordered to lay aside their own quarrels and work together under the king. Sheriffs were told to stay in their county towns ready for the signal. All knights, squires and gentlemen

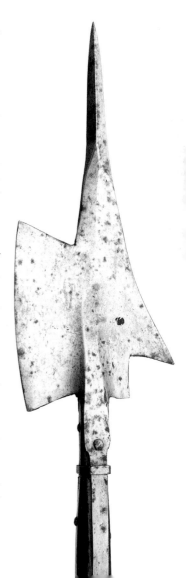

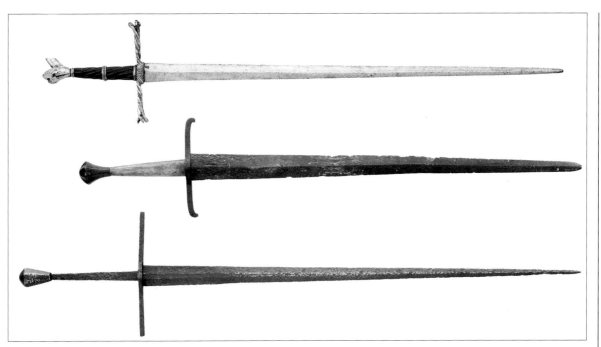

were to hold themselves in readiness at an hour's notice, the penalty for disobeying this instruction being the loss of life, lands and goods. Officers were to muster the able-bodied men of their bailiwicks, see them well horsed and harnessed, and collect money for their wages. The commissions had been set up in December and Richard had already had to apply forced loans on churchmen and pawn silver plate and jewels to London merchants in order to raise money.

There is little detail of the preparations of Henry Tudor, and the royal proclamation may simply reflect the fact that an invasion force was now actively gathering in France. Through late spring and early summer last-minute preparations were under way, as Henry sent agents across the Channel to firm up commitments by sympathisers and to win over others. *The Song of Lady Bessy* states that Lord Stanley, Sir William Stanley and Gilbert Talbot met together on 3 May and pledged to support Henry to the throne. The ballad also relates, however inaccurately, that when the news was conveyed to Henry by Sir Humphrey Brereton, the pretender was inspired enough to ask Charles VIII one last time for more help, and to launch the invasion plans. Certainly in early June Henry had committed himself to invade and at about this time several sympathisers of rank are also known to have disappeared into sanctuary, no doubt prematurely warned of coming events. John Morgan sent a message that Rhys ap Thomas and John Savage were ready to assist, and that Reginald Bray had collected a substantial sum of money with which to buy soldiers.

Morgan advised Henry to set out for Wales as soon as possible. The time for invasion was ripe.

The invasion force was hardly inspiring in composition. It is true that there were a number of notable commanders: Oxford and Pembroke, Sir Edward Woodville, former admiral of England, and the Bishop of Exeter. Several other worthy fighting men had fled to Henry's court, such as Richard Edgecombe and Richard Guildford, who was keen to work with artillery. Added to these was James Blount and the soldiers who had followed him from the garrison at Hammes. However, this only amounted to perhaps 500 men and probably less. Although it is not known exactly how many troops were actually supplied by Charles VIII, a large percentage of Henry's force, perhaps as many as 4,000 men, was composed of French mercenaries. Philibert de Chandée, the principal captain, appears to have been a close friend of Henry himself. A unit of gunners, plus some armourers and other specialists had come to the camp. The comments of Commines that some of the Frenchmen were rabble is unlikely to be accurate. Scottish tradition has Bernard Stuart and Alexander Bruce serving with units of Scottish troops who were with

Henry Tudor stands on the clifftop above Mill Bay, having climbed up from the beach-head. Below, his ships lay at anchor. They are mainly small cogs with fore-castles and stern-castles, though it is not known exactly what types of vessel or how many he in fact had at his disposal. The inlet, the first on the north side of Milford Haven, provided a sheltered spot for his small flotilla. Before him lay the small castle of Dale, which his troops are about to advance on and attack. Having met no other opposition, the small army of perhaps some 4,000 men made camp on the heights before setting off next morning.

GRAHAM TURNER '99

the French army. However it was viewed, the invasion force was not strong in numbers, though as Commines pointed out, the number of ships and amount of supplies tended to dictate numbers in any case. Nevertheless, Henry's gallant band would have to face the might of what some continental writers regarded as the most powerful English king of recent years.

Henry and his small fleet set out from Harfleur on the Seine estuary on Monday 1 August. It is not known why this particular date was chosen but it is probable that circumstances and fair weather determined their departure. Nor is it known how many ships comprised the flotilla. Unlike the storms that beset the invasion two years earlier, this time the ships rode with a gentle south wind. They coasted north-westwards along the Channel for several days without encountering any obvious problems. Finally, on Sunday 7 August, the rocky coastline of Pembrokeshire hove into view. Though the Crowland chronicler has 1 August as the date, this does not seem tenable. This area was probably the best place for a landing. For one thing it was a quiet, rugged coast supplied with inlets safe from the worst weather, and it was well away from the centre of royal authority. Secondly, it would give Henry a chance to enlarge his army with new recruits. He had been cultivating his 'Welshness' in the hope that he could persuade the people of the country to welcome his invasion and actively send support in the form of armed men. He was known in Pembrokeshire from his years before exile, and his uncle Jasper Tudor had influence as Earl of Pembroke. Other supporters like the Morgan brothers had done their best to pave the way for the invasion. It is hard to tell how Henry felt, seeing the Welsh coast for the first time in 15 years. How would the inhabitants react?

A stone ball, perhaps a cannon ball, dug up on the battlefield. It is difficult to say whether any balls found, particularly cast-iron examples, came from this battle or from the skirmish during the English Civil War of the mid-17th century.

A Milanese barbut of about 1460, stamped with the Milanese maker's marks. (By courtesy of the Trustees of the Armouries)

The fleet waited until sunset before it nuzzled into the wide inlet of Milford Haven, at that time a deserted landscape lacking the town of the same name that would be founded in the 18th century. Mill Bay lay half a mile across the narrow peninsula of St Ann's Head. It was the first sheltered cove on the western side, with a stretch of sand unlike the other shingle beaches. Here the ships dropped anchor, out of sight of Dale Castle on the high ground beyond, which Henry feared might be held against him. When he disembarked he knelt on the sand and prayed, beginning with the words from the psalm: 'Judge me, O Lord, and determine my cause'. Around him the troops swarmed

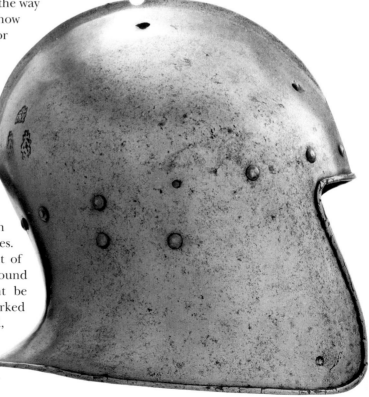

from the ships and established a beachhead. Some marched up the hill and on to the headland to attack Dale Castle, a small fortification that probably fell within hours. Henry, so local tradition has it, clambered up close by Brunt Farm, given the name from his remark that it was a 'brunt' place, meaning in English 'hard ground' or in Welsh a 'foul spot'. A small force may have landed at Angle on the opposite side of the haven, intending to oppose Pembroke.

With no enemy nearby, and Dale Castle secure, the invaders made camp for the night. That evening and the following morning Henry knighted a number of his followers: Philibert de Chandée, Edward Courtenay, later Earl of Devon, John Welles, John Cheney, Edward Poynings, John Fortescue, James Blount and David Owen. It helped to boost morale. It is worth noting that *Lady Bessy* says that Henry advised the Stanleys to expect him at Michaelmas, a month later than the actual invasion. Another comment in the ballad shows Sir William Stanley working out the sea route of the invaders from the wind direction, so it may have been thought that the weather would be more favourable then. Again, it might have made more sense to wait longer in order to allow the summer heat to harden the muddy passes which the invaders would march through in central Wales. It would also allow any sympathisers more time to raise their followers. Though there were no enemies, there were few friends to hand either. After all the negotiations, the reception must have been a huge anti-climax.

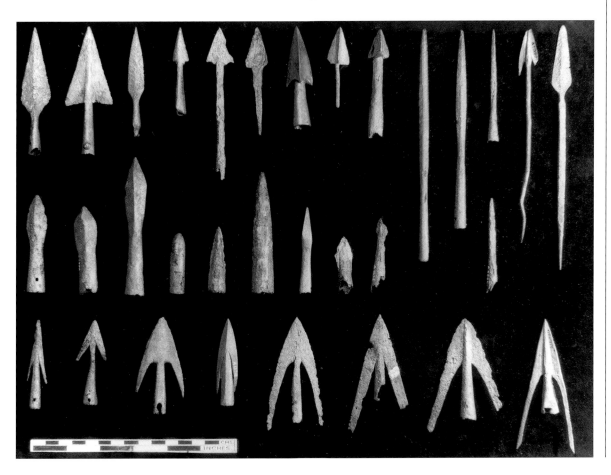

Arrowheads of various types. The broadheads (bottom right), with their barbs to prevent them falling out and their long cutting surfaces, were mainly for hunting but easily cut through flesh and were used to shoot horses. The long bodkins (top right) could even bore several centimetres through plate armour, provided they did not glance off. The commonest general purpose head is the fourth from left on the bottom row. The centre row comprises mainly crossbow heads. (Museum of London)

THE MARCH TO BOSWORTH

The advance through Wales

Henry's army seemed very much alone. Though it is possible that minor local gentry greeted the invaders, no major leaders had appeared to swell his numbers. That same Monday, 8 August, Henry marched the ten miles north-eastwards to Haverfordwest, which lay on a hill overlooking the River Cleddau and was itself overlooked by the old castle. Several miles beyond, Jasper Tudor's influence bore fruit when Henry received Arnold Butler with messages of support from Pembroke on the opposite side of Milford Haven, and probably some men also. The story that Rhys ap Thomas greeted Henry at Dale, and made speeches while the French soldiers stayed in their ships, must be ignored; indeed, there were now rumours that he was actively raising royal troops and, to make matters worse, that Walter Herbert was about to descend from Carmarthen further east. There had been suggestions that both men might be brought over to his side and the possible threat from Herbert eased when a local gentleman, William ap Griffith, arrived to join them with part of the Carmarthenshire muster on 9 August. John Morgan also brought a few soldiers. Henry now marched north-westward from Cardigan, along the coast road through Llanbadarnfawr and then on to Machynlleth. A letter from Henry, discovered a few years ago, is dated 14 August at Machynlleth, showing that the march through Wales was even slower than previously supposed as he endeavoured to gather support and plan his movements. According to local tradition, he was met at Mathafarn outside Machynlleth by the famous poet Davydd Llwyd, who prophesied victory for Henry. He now turned inland, passing through the Cambrian Mountains of central Wales. Letters of encouragement had been sent to a number of hopeful relatives and adherents, and small detachments of Welsh supporters probably joined the rebels as they progressed through the country, a supposition supported by the fact that a number of local gentry and yeomen were rewarded later. The work of the Welsh bard Robin Ddu that spoke of Henry and the trust the nation placed in him, had already been ingested by many.

Yet Henry still could not know just how many men would actually rally to his standards, despite his claim to being Prince of Wales and his uncle's title of Earl of Pembroke. He still had no idea of the sympathies of either Rhys ap Thomas or Walter Herbert. Both had, in addition to their own followers, mustered troops from the southern counties, and were shadowing the little rebel army along inland routes. If their intention was friendly, this movement could simply be a trick to give the king the impression that his forces were in control of the situation. If not, Henry knew he would be in extreme danger. Rhys had been won over to the Lancastrian cause but King Richard, growing suspicious, had demanded his young son as hostage plus an oath of allegiance. Rhys had

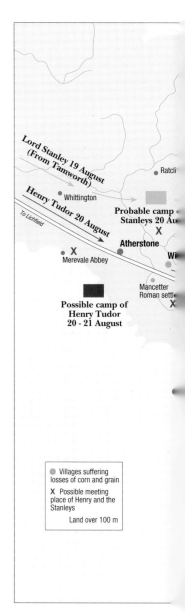

Villages suffering losses of corn and grain

X Possible meeting place of Henry and the Stanleys

Land over 100 m

refused his son on the grounds that he was too young and now would have to tread with caution.

Even if Rhys proved friendly, the Earl of Huntingdon further east was not. However, the ballad tradition implies that Henry always intended to head north and west, both to draw in the Welsh leaders from the centre of the country and to make contact with the Stanleys and supporters in the north-west of England. At the moment he still had no reassurances of help from his step-father, Lord Stanley, and he must have been relieved when, in the vicinity of Newtown or a little further east, Rhys ap Thomas finally showed his hand and joined the invading army. He is said to have been offered the lieutenancy of Wales to finally lure him over, but Henry never forgot the worry he had been put through and the

POSSIBLE MOVEMENTS OF THE ARMIES CONVERGING ON BOSWORTH, 19–21 AUGUST 1485

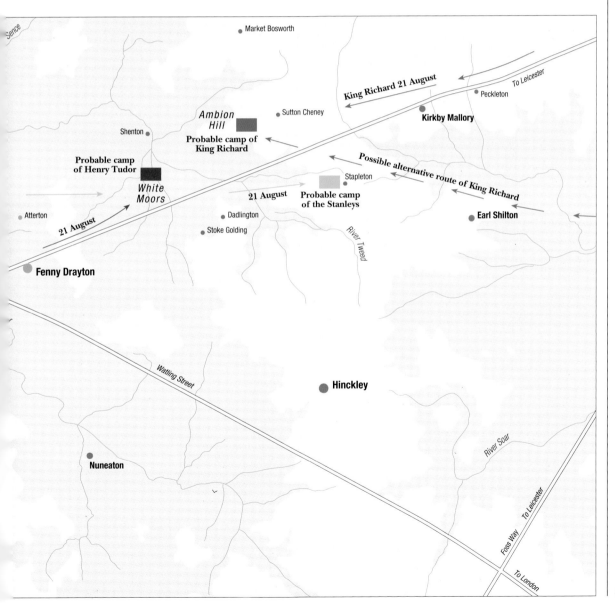

attainment of great rank would elude Rhys. His force was probably as large as all Henry's existing Welsh contingents put together and included men such as Philip ap Howel, whose wife had been Henry's nurse. Richard ap Howel of Mostyn also arrived. Many of these men would be rewarded later by a grateful Henry. Walter Herbert also rode in, either at the same time or soon afterwards, with men from south-east Wales. When Henry reached Long Mountain, near Welshpool, he was joined by men from North Wales, including some of his own kinsmen and chieftains such as Rhys Fawr ap Maredudd, who would perform such deeds at Bosworth that he would become part of Welsh legend. Henry marched down the Severn Valley and over the English border probably on about 15 or 16 August, in the direction of Shrewsbury. He knew that Richard must by now be gathering his forces ready to destroy this second invasion of his realm.

The king alerted

Richard was at Beskwood Lodge near Nottingham, from where he hunted in Sherwood Forest, when he was informed on 11 August that Henry Tudor had landed. One of the king's agents, Richard Williams, Constable of Pembroke Castle, had not defected and is most probably the person responsible for the message reaching the king so fast – 200 miles only four days after the landfall. The first report seems to have contained the information that the rebels had landed at Angle, which lies on the east side of Milford Haven. The ships were probably seen approaching the Haven and the message sent off in haste, as soon as it was decided that the invader was too large to be withstood alone. Less likely is the explanation that someone could have misunderstood the signal beacons.

Polydore Vergil asserts that when he was informed of the landing, Richard was dismissive of the invaders and confident that they could be contained by his troops in Wales. After all, had he not already dealt with one invasion in his reign and beaten it with relative ease? The enemy was being followed by what the king still assumed were loyal captains, and was not heading directly across into England. Certainly Richard celebrated the Assumption of the Blessed Virgin Mary on 15 August, postponing any warlike measures. However, he had also issued orders to his nobles, lesser lords and gentry, and the sheriffs and commissioners of array were swiftly directed to raise their men. The king soon learned that his so-called subject Rhys ap Thomas had gone over to the enemy and that, swollen in numbers, the rebel army was now at large in England. Worse still, it turned out that Shrewsbury had welcomed them in. This doubled his determination to act. The Wars of the Roses had shown that the sooner an opponent could be confronted, the less time he had for collecting additional recruits. The Duke of Norfolk

Scarborough Castle, on the north Yorkshire coast, where Anne Neville stayed during the invasion scare of 1483 and from whose port Richard's fleet sailed.

Bodiam Castle. This almost picturesque 14th-century castle deep in the heart of Sussex was held against Richard by the southern rebels in 1483. As the revolt collapsed, it was besieged by royal forces and surrendered.

had received orders to mobilise, his men coming together at Bury St Edmunds on the evening of 16 August. The king already had a large number of lords with him in Nottingham, such as the Earl of Lincoln, Lord Scrope and Lord Strange. Demands also went north, to Percy of Northumberland and the Stanleys. On 16 August the citizens of York sent to ask what the king wanted them to do, which must have given Richard pause for thought. Percy should have dealt with that, and was obviously more interested in surrounding himself with his own personal followers, rather than with men such as those in York, with close ties to Richard. Perhaps more worrying, there was little movement from Lord Stanley, despite the fact that his own son Lord Strange was being held by Richard as surety for his untrustworthy father.

The advance across England

Henry Tudor had reached Shrewsbury on 15 or 16 August and found the gates shut for the night. Having gone through this formality, they were opened by the bailiff, John Mitton, after the 'diligent' labour of Richard Crompe. However, though Henry might be received within the walls, there was no cordial welcome nor, more importantly, ostensible aid in manpower. He had already sent letters to his mother, Margaret Beaufort, and to the Stanley brothers, Talbot and others, in which he mentioned his plans to cross the Severn and move towards London. He had received in reply some welcome cash and words of support, but not men. He set out, not in fact directly for London via Watling Street, but rather eastwards, presumably hoping to contact English sympathisers, notably the Stanleys. He probably reached Newport (Shropshire) the same day. Here, at last, he was joined by Gilbert Talbot with perhaps 500 men, the first overt signal from a substantial English ally. Talbot may also have provided Henry with information about the whereabouts of his stepfather, Lord Stanley. Henry moved on to Stafford, where, on the evening of 16 or perhaps 17 August, Sir William Stanley finally rode into the camp with a small escort. No one knows what was said, and Stanley rode out again soon afterwards. It seems likely that he asked Henry to slow down his advance, since the march from here on was not nearly as swift as before. The 150 miles from Dale to Shrewsbury, over difficult terrain, had been traversed in little more than a week, but it would take nearly another week to move through Stafford to Lichfield, 50 miles on good roads. The Stanleys needed time to move their own forces in front of Henry, as though shadowing him for the king, but this would also provide a screen behind which the rebels could acquire as many reinforcements as they could, while using the slow pace to rest their weary soldiers.

King Richard crosses Bow Bridge as he leaves Leicester on 21 August to confront Henry Tudor. The king wears full armour of west European style. He also proclaims his sovereignty in the gold circlet, possibly a deliberate imitation of his forebear, Henry V, who wore a crown round his helmet when he won the battle of Agincourt. Behind him are borne his personal banner with the royal arms and his standard bearing the emblem of the white boar. The Duke of Norfolk probably rode with his troops in front and Northumberland in rear. Behind is the Franciscan Friary in which Richard would eventually be laid.

GRAHAM TURNER

Henry needed the Stanleys and their impressive forces. Without them his prospects of successfully opposing a royal army were slim. He was probably pondering over this when he found himself detached from the army as it moved from Lichfield to Tamworth, and realised that he was lost in enemy territory with about 20 men. Henry spent what must have been a hair-raising night before he managed to locate the army next morning, which was on the point of breaking up amid rumours that he had fled. Henry shrugged off his escapade by saying he had gone to seek out some potential supporters. Sir Thomas Bourchier and Sir Walter Hungerford joined Henry at about this time, having deserted Brackenbury's force at Stony Stratford. This may have caused some skirmishing as they crossed Stanley lines, since chroniclers mention that Sir William Stanley believed his brother to be under attack during this period. Alternatively, Richard Boughton, Sheriff of Warwickshire and Leicestershire, killed on 20 August, possibly died in combat with these deserters or, less likely, with Lord Stanley's men.

Though actually a depiction of English troops invading France during the Hundred Years War, this late 15th-century illumination provides a good illustration of the ships and men that Henry Tudor would have used. (By permission of the British Library, MS. Royal 18 E.i f.103v)

The route of the Stanleys

The Stanley brothers had begun to array their men before the royal summons arrived, since word of Henry's landing had reached them before it reached King Richard. According to *Lady Bessy*, they rode out on Monday 15 August. Lord Stanley left Lathom and struck out for Newcastle-under-Lyme, gathering men from Warrington and several other rallying places en route. His brother left Holt and marched to Nantwich. Some dialogue may well have passed between them, since their joint movements seem to have been in some ways co-ordinated. Sir William moved slowly to Stone, from which he rode to his meeting with Henry. On 20 or perhaps 21 August he organised a reception for the pretender at Lichfield, complete with cannon and military honours. Lord Stanley had arrived there on 17 August but rode out again days before Henry arrived, as though keeping ahead of the invaders. He simply could not be seen to be joining his stepson, if he wanted his own son, Lord Strange, to remain safe. His brother, Sir William Stanley, was not constrained by such duress. By 19 August Lord Stanley was close by Atherstone, from where he might appear to deny the invaders the road to London. However, he was also blocking Watling Street and might also deny King Richard access to the rebels.

By the evening of 20 August, Henry Tudor had arrived at Atherstone. He may have set up quarters in the nearby Cistercian abbey of Merevale, rather than the Three Tuns inn of local tradition. He later recompensed the abbey for damage to its lands, presumably by his troops. The Stanleys may have camped for the night in the area bounded by the conjunction of the Sence and Anker rivers, which may be the dale mentioned in the prose version of the *Ballad of Bosworth Field*. The following day, according to the *Ballad*, Henry met the Stanleys out of a 'fforrest syde', probably crossing north over the Anker from the camp south of Atherstone town. The Stanleys may have later moved east to Stapleton, perhaps being responsible for the earthworks dug there. Soon after nightfall Sir John Savage, Sir Brian Sandford and Sir Simon Digby defected from the King's army and joined Henry. John Hardwick, a local gentleman who offered his services as a guide, may well have suggested White Moors as a camp; Henry probably moved his forces there for the night. Certainly, recompense was later given to the villages of Witherley, Atterton, Fenny Drayton and Mancetter for loss of corn taken 'by us and our companye at oure late victorious feld'. This, together with other inferences, such as the Croyland chronicler's mention of the battle being fought near Merevale and John Rous's reference to it on the borders of Warwickshire and Leicestershire, have led David Starkey and Margaret Condon to suggest that the actual battle may have taken place near Merevale.

Richard marches

On 20 August Richard left Nottingham in battle formation, the baggage and arms in the centre, followed by the king and his household. Reaching Leicester by sunset, Richard is said to have taken residence in the White Boar inn. Norfolk had probably already arrived and Brackenbury soon after. On 21 August Northumberland arrived, and the king rode over Bow Bridge westwards out of the city. Richard presumably marched towards Leicester forest down the Roman road to Watling Street, in order to block Henry's route to London. His scurriers had learnt that the enemy was at Atherstone, so Richard left the Roman road at some point near Sutton Cheney. However, if the eastern part of the Roman road near Leicester had virtually disappeared, Richard may instead have crossed the forest chase and picked up an ancient track below Earl Shilton, which led across Ambion Hill. The royal host camped on or near that hill.

A view of St Ann's Head, the entrance to Milford Haven. Mill Bay is to the right. Dale Castle lies out of view beyond the top left corner. (Aerofilms Ltd)

THE BATTLE

The Field of Bosworth

Sentries and spies were about during the night. One later (highly unlikely) story relates how Richard toured his lines and found a sentry asleep. Drawing his knife he slew the man on the spot with the remark: 'I find him asleep and I leave him asleep'.

The sun rose at about 05.15 hours, Richard had not, it seems, slept well. The Crowland chronicler explains that he had seen dreadful visions in the night, in which he was surrounded by demons. It might be thought that the Tudor writers would see this as the prelude to the death of an evil tyrant, but Polydore Vergil, with his Renaissance intuition, attributes it to a guilty conscience rather than a celestial warning. Perhaps rather unwisely Richard told his companions about the dreams, though according to the Crowland chronicler his appearance would have in any case suggested something was wrong: 'He consequently presented a countenance which, always drawn, was on this occasion more livid and ghastly than usual.'

The king made the point that whoever won the battle would cause the destruction of England; if Richard won he would crush all the traitors who had opposed him, while if Henry Tudor was victorious he would do much the same thing. For the first time in the Wars of the Roses, a king and a challenger for the crown faced each other in the field.

The battlefield

One of the earliest references to the battle comes in the *York House Book* entry for 23 August 1485, with a mention of 'John Sponer, send unto the feld of Redemore to bring tidinges frome the same

The garter stall plate of Francis, Viscount Lovell. Notice the crest of a dog, alluded to in Collingbourne's rhyme. (Reproduced by permission of the Dean and Canons of Windsor)

to the Citie'. 'Redmore' or 'Redemore' has been variously interpreted as alluding to the red clay of the soil (note the name 'White Moors' for Henry's probable camp) or to the 'reed moor', especially (according to Foss) the area beyond the Sence Brook towards Dadlington. The first mention of 'Redemor' appears in the Hinckley-Lyre agreement of 1283, only surviving as a 19th-century copy of an 18th-century transcript. It refers to meadow in Redemor in the fields of Dadlington, though in fact it may well mean in that part of Redemor in the fields of Dadlington. A late 15th-century note to a genealogical table refers to the battle at 'Brownehethe', probably a corruption of 'red moor' perhaps via the Welsh 'rhos goch'. The first mention of Bosworth as the name for the

BOSWORTH FIELD, 22 AUGUST 1485

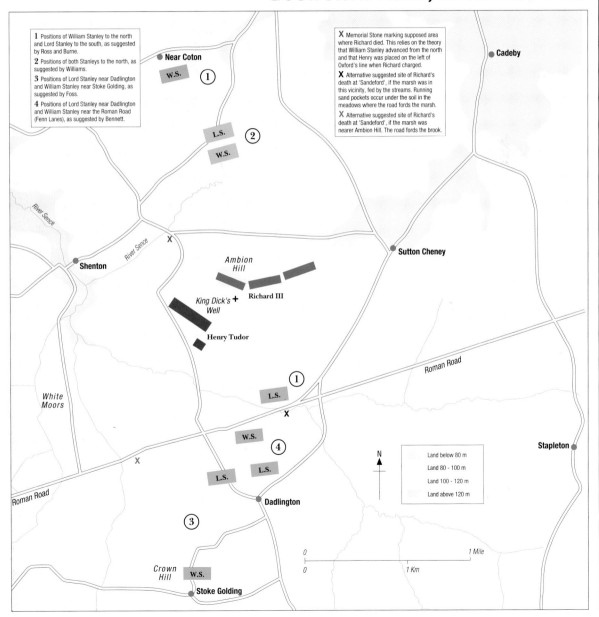

1 Positions of William Stanley to the north and Lord Stanley to the south, as suggested by Ross and Burne.

2 Positions of both Stanleys to the north, as suggested by Williams.

3 Positions of Lord Stanley near Dadlington and William Stanley near Stoke Golding, as suggested by Foss.

4 Positions of Lord Stanley near Dadlington and William Stanley near the Roman Road (Fenn Lanes), as suggested by Bennett.

X Memorial Stone marking supposed area where Richard died. This relies on the theory that William Stanley advanced from the north and that Henry was placed on the left of Oxford's line when Richard charged.

X Alternative suggested site of Richard's death at 'Sandeford', if the marsh was in this vicinity, fed by the streams. Running sand pockets occur under the soil in the meadows where the road fords the marsh.

X Alternative suggested site of Richard's death at 'Sandeford', if the marsh was nearer Ambion Hill. The road fords the brook.

Near Coton

W.S. ①

L.S. ②

W.S.

Cadeby

River Sence

River Sence

Shenton

X

Ambion Hill

Richard III

King Dick's Well +

Henry Tudor

Sutton Cheney

Roman Road

White Moors

L.S. ①

X

W.S.

④

L.S. L.S.

X

Dadlington

③

Stapleton

N

Land below 80 m
Land 80 - 100 m
Land 100 - 120 m
Land above 120 m

Roman Road

Crown Hill

W.S.

Stoke Golding

0 ——————— 1 Mile
0 ——————— 1 Km

battle is found in the *Great Chronicle of London*, where it takes place in the 'ffyeldys adjoynant', to be followed in 1516 by *Fabyan's Chronicle*, probably because Bosworth was the nearest large village. The earliest map reference, Christopher Saxton's map of Leicestershire and Warwickshire, dated 1576, shows an oval area marked as 'King Ric. feld'. It is on this example that subsequent maps were based, and shows an area called the Sence Brook. In 1610 John Speed, rightly or wrongly, added the name 'Red More' to his map, placing it north of the stream.

From Sutton Cheney a ridge of high ground spread westwards past a deserted hamlet before sloping down to a level area across which flowed the Sence Brook. This was known as Ambion Hill, first noted in connection with the battle by Holinshed, who refers to 'Anne Beame' ((?)'one tree'). Two miles to the north was the spire of Bosworth village church. William Burton, in his description of Leicestershire of 1622, noted the battlefield as three miles from Bosworth – nearer Dadlington – but in his revisions of 1642 subsequently changed it to two miles. To the west lay Shenton and, further to the left, the distant camp fires of Henry Tudor on the slopes of White Moors. At the bottom of the slope, on the southern side, the old Roman road from Leicester ran past on its way to Watling Street. Beyond the road, on rising ground, stood Stoke Golding church. At the foot of the slope of Ambion Hill lay a large area of marshy ground. The exact whereabouts and extent of this marsh have been the subject of endless debate, since the land was drained and enclosed in the 16th century ('by reason of ditches cast, it is growne to be firme ground', notes Holinshed in the 1570s), and Ambion Wood now stands at the foot of the slope on the southern side. Hutton, who walked the field in the 18th century, mentioned that another marsh extended round the hill to the east. The original marsh, fed from several springs and from the Sence Brook, probably formed part of a much larger area of boggy ground; indeed, the area in the wood can still be boggy. Peter Foss states

Richard's 'Castle of Care', a reconstruction of Nottingham Castle, seen from the north, as it probably looked in 1485. Perched on its cliff, the residential buildings erected by Edward IV are on the left; the main gate leading to the town is at centre rear. (Nottingham Civic Society and the Thoroton Society)

The main gatehouse of Nottingham Castle, heavily restored. Much of the original castle has been destroyed.

that this is caused by the water table and by ridge and furrow ploughing under the present wood, which holds water in the furrows. Attempts have been made to site the marsh further off, either closer to the brook or else beyond it. Arguments for both cases, based on soil conditions and place-name derivations, can be put forward. However, a point worth noting in locating the marsh is the comment of Vergil. Richard, he says, ordered Norfolk's men to attack as soon as the enemy was past the marsh. Assuming that his army was on the crest of Ambion Hill and that an archery contest opened proceedings, the marsh would be little more than an extreme bowshot from the ridge, this was about 300 metres. Some writers (notably Peter Foss) have suggested that the marsh was well to the south-west of the Sence. If Oxford then passed beyond it to the foot of Ambion Hill, not only would this contradict Vergil's comment about Norfolk's immediate assault, it would leave Oxford's right flank wide open to an attack by the king's division. It may be argued that Richard brought his army down from the hill before the battle, but that would, from the start, leave Northumberland's division way back on the heights (where all agreed he stayed) in a blatant show of treachery. Moreover, if there had earlier been confusion in its camp could Richard's army have had time to advance down and across the Sence, if it was to

Pembroke Castle, on the opposite side of Milford Haven. Henry Tudor was born here on 28 January 1457, when his uncle, Jasper Tudor, was Earl of Pembroke. Having lost the castle to the Herberts, it became a potential threat to the invaders, although Herbert did not trouble them.

Royal gunners open fire from the crest of Ambion Hill at the beginning of the battle of Bosworth. The barrels are made from welded iron staves bound with hoops and the guns are breech-loaded, provided with ready-charged chambers. Held in place by a wedge, this allowed swift reloading but the rather poor fit meant loss of power from escaping gases. The serpentine powder tended to settle out into its constituent parts but these 'hoop and stave' barrels were not strong enough for the more reliable but powerful corned powder then coming into use. These guns have a split trail to elevate or depress the barrel. Cast-iron balls, though mentioned in 1490, would be exceedingly rare until the 16th century and it is likely that those found at Bosworth are actually from the Civil War skirmish which took place in the 17th century. *The Ballad of Bosworth Field* also mentions springalds, torsion catapults that shot large bolts.

attack Oxford as he passed the marsh? What would the advantage be in bringing a large army down on to level ground when some of it would face a bog? Vegetius points out the merits of holding high ground, and Richard was well versed in his advice. In addition, on a still day his archers would gain a slight advantage in range by standing on a hill, and it is worth noting that *The Rose of England* mentions how Oxford by his marching tried to gain the advantage of sun and wind. Having the sun behind blinds an opposing force to incoming arrows; the wind behind slightly shortens the range of enemy shafts.

Richard probably rode to the brow of Ambion Hill to watch for the advancing enemy. On his return he found the camp in a state of confusion. The Crowland chronicler describes how no chaplain could be found to perform divine service for the king. The story is somewhat echoed in two other early sources: one is in a book of miracles compiled

by Lord Morley, who recalls the story of one Bigod, a carver for Richard who fought for him in the battle. Bigod told how 'when his chaplain had one thing ready, evermore they wanted another, when they had wine they lacked bread'. The delay in divine service would mean a delay also in breakfast, and with the enemy advance the latter was then cancelled. The second source, *The Ballad of Bosworth Field*, has Sir William Stanley promise that he will give Richard a breakfast he will not forget. Perhaps he took the opportunity to drink fresh water from the spring on the south-east slope which has traditionally become known as 'King Richard's Well'.

The rebel deployment

To compound the confusion, it appears that Henry Tudor was already advancing purposefully from his camp on White Moors. Henry was awake before dawn. Unlike his adversary, he managed to hear Mass and partake of breakfast. Then his force of perhaps 5,000 men began its advance towards the huge royal army. The invading host, though easy enough to manoeuvre compared to the enemy on the hill, was also worryingly small. Henry decided to commit most of his men in a single large division or 'battle' and place it under command of the Earl of Oxford. This was the best choice, given Oxford's reputation and experience.

We simply do not know in detail how the division was composed, but it must have contained Welsh archers, presumably under Rhys ap Thomas. Similarly French and Scottish mercenaries would have been commanded by Philbert de Chandée and Bernard Stuart respectively. Most English men-at-arms were probably placed in a smaller body on each wing, where stood (says Vergil) on the right, Gilbert Talbot, and on the left, John Savage. While this impressive body marched in front, Henry brought up the rear with a small band of retainers, including the Earl of Pembroke, the Bishop of Exeter, Sir John Cheney and an elite guard. Close by, William Brandon bore Henry's standard, the red dragon floating on its background of white and green.

Richard's deployment

Richard, meanwhile, was now hurriedly trying to array his troops in line of battle. Compared to his enemy, his forces were large, and it required some effort to produce an ordered front on what was a relatively cramped hilltop. It would appear that, considering the paucity of numbers in the invading army, Richard was somewhat surprised to find Henry marching boldly forward in the valley below, and the king was not as prepared as he should have been. It

A commission of array from Richard III, sent from Nottingham and dated 22 June 1485. (By permission of the British Library, MS. Harleian 433, f.220)

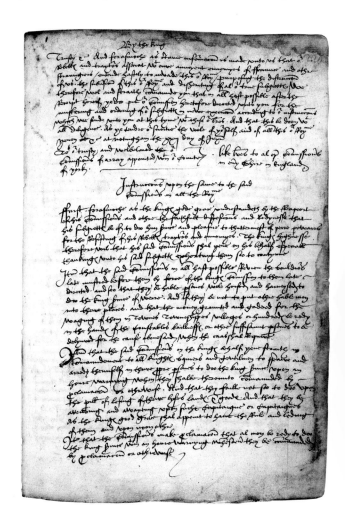

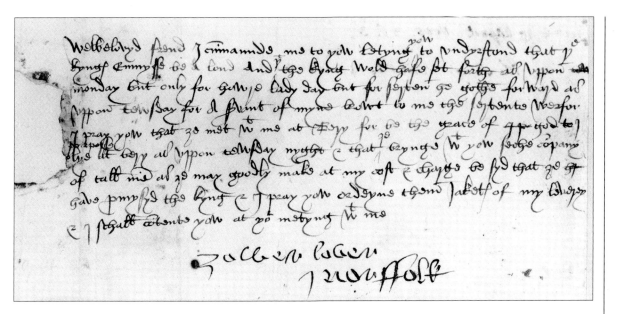

A letter from the Duke of Norfolk to John Paston, ordering him to meet him on 16 August at the muster at Bury St Edmunds with his quota as promised to the king, together with 'such company of tall men as ye may goodly make at my expense and charge'. It is signed 'your lover [i.e. well-wisher] J. Norffolk'. (By permission of the British Library, MS. Add. 43490, f.53)

may be that he expected Henry to wait, that a show of strength by the royalist army would be enough to dishearten the invaders, especially the mercenaries, who saw no profit in defeat. This might perhaps encourage numbers to desert before a blow was struck. Even if the invading army held its ground, the first onslaught down the slope would propel Henry's men from the field in ignominious flight. As Richard now realised, this did not seem quite as likely as he had perhaps imagined.

The royalists now began to form themselves into divisions or 'battles'. It is fairly safe to propose that three battles were formed. Though such a formation – vanguard, main body and rearguard – was commonly favoured by medieval commanders there is no direct evidence for this at Bosworth. However, the chroniclers give the impression that three natural divisions can be made out, one under the Duke of Norfolk, another under Richard himself, and the third under the Earl of Northumberland. Beyond this it becomes a clouded issue; indeed, even the three battles are only mentioned in the English translations of Vergil, who in the original version simply speaks of the Duke of Norfolk commanding the archers at the front of a long battle-line. Molinet, probably the best source for this, describes a vanguard of about 11,000-12,000 men, under the joint command of Norfolk and Brackenbury. Lindsay has it under Stanley and Brackenbury, while de Valera speaks of a van of 7,000 men commanded by the 'grand chamberlain', with a left wing under somebody named 'Tamerlant'. This may well be a reference to Lord Stanley and, together with the mention by Lindsay and other factors, will have some bearing on the placement of Stanley's troops at the start of the battle.

This apart, we are still left with no certain knowledge of how these three divisions were deployed. It would appear that Norfolk did indeed have command (or joint command) of a division, the vanguard, though we are not told whether the vanguard was on the right of the line with King Richard to its left, or whether the vanguard filled the entire front of the hill on the south-west, with Richard behind. Either way, the first troops of Richard's battle to reach the crest, under Sir Robert

THE ADVANCE, 22 AUGUST 1485

Having roused at dawn the small army of Henry Tudor begins to move from its campsite at White Moors, probably around 07.00. Lord Stanley and Sir William Stanley were encamped near Stapleton and are now moving towards the battlefield, but still hold back from committing themselves. On, or near, Ambion Hill, King Richard is somewhat surprised that the enemy is advancing, and endeavours to order his battles.

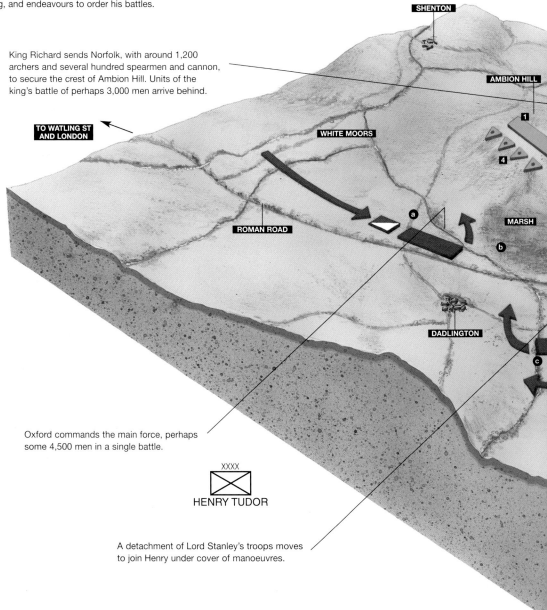

King Richard sends Norfolk, with around 1,200 archers and several hundred spearmen and cannon, to secure the crest of Ambion Hill. Units of the king's battle of perhaps 3,000 men arrive behind.

SHENTON

AMBION HILL

TO WATLING ST AND LONDON

WHITE MOORS

1

4

ROMAN ROAD

a

b

MARSH

DADLINGTON

c

Oxford commands the main force, perhaps some 4,500 men in a single battle.

XXXX

HENRY TUDOR

A detachment of Lord Stanley's troops moves to join Henry under cover of manoeuvres.

REBELS		RICARDIANS	
a	Henry Tudor	1	Norfolk
b	Oxford	2	Richard III
c	Sir William Stanley	3	Northumberland
d	Lord Stanley	4	Ricardian Artillery

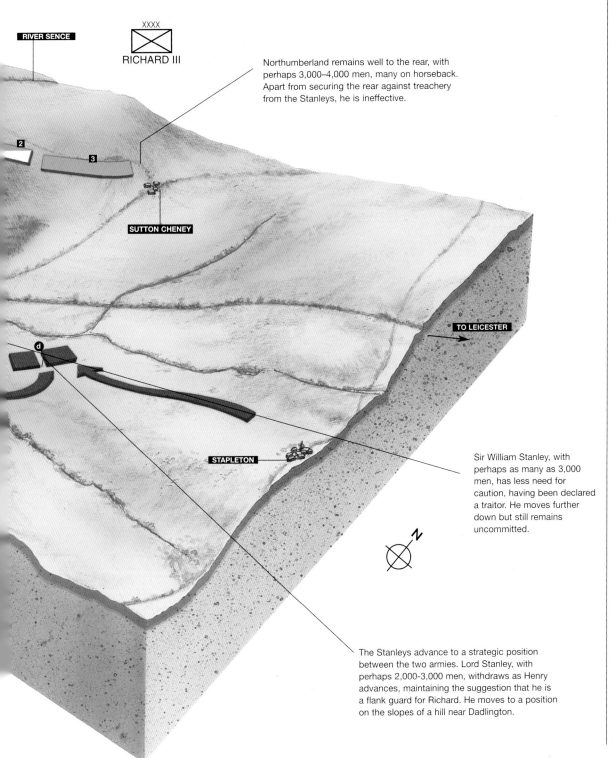

RIVER SENCE

XXXX
RICHARD III

Northumberland remains well to the rear, with perhaps 3,000–4,000 men, many on horseback. Apart from securing the rear against treachery from the Stanleys, he is ineffective.

2

3

SUTTON CHENEY

TO LEICESTER

d

STAPLETON

N

Sir William Stanley, with perhaps as many as 3,000 men, has less need for caution, having been declared a traitor. He moves further down but still remains uncommitted.

The Stanleys advance to a strategic position between the two armies. Lord Stanley, with perhaps 2,000-3,000 men, withdraws as Henry advances, maintaining the suggestion that he is a flank guard for Richard. He moves to a position on the slopes of a hill near Dadlington.

The house in Shrewsbury where, according to tradition, Henry Tudor stayed during his march. There is little hard evidence to support the story.

Brackenbury, reinforced Norfolk's men. It seems likely that wherever the other two battles were placed, Northumberland was set at the right or, more probably, to the rear of Richard's battle, as noted by the Crowland chronicler and by Molinet.

However the actual forces were deployed, it seems that the hilltop was alive with armed men. Vergil alludes to Norfolk's troops spread in a line, the soldiers packed together. He mentions that this division consisted of both horse and foot, with the archers in the front ranks. Horsemen would certainly be packed close together to enable them to advance like a steel steamroller bristling with lances, which would be levelled as they spurred to a gallop before shock. Vergil then describes Richard's select force as being to the rear of this division. Lindsay, though a later chronicler, makes the connection between Brackenbury and the cannon in the vanguard. As lieutenant of the Tower of London, says Lindsay, he was captain of the ordnance, a not unlikely situation given that the

The church of St Mary, originally the chapel outside the gate of the Cistercian abbey at Merevale, near Atherstone. Henry's army probably camped on lands owned by the abbey. He himself may have stayed at the abbey, and perhaps met Lord Stanley somewhere in the area, though other sites are possible.

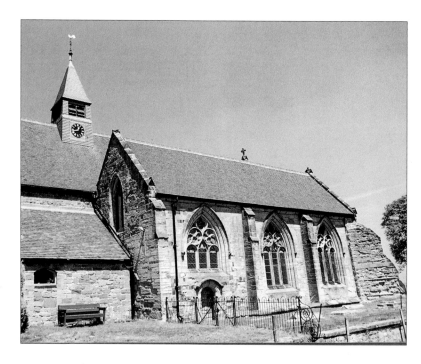

Bow Bridge, on the road over the River Soar out of Leicester. The present structure, built in 1862, replaced the medieval structure, which was pulled down the previous year. The plaque commemorates the march of Richard's army across the bridge on the way to Bosworth. He is supposed to have struck his spur against a stone on the bridge, and a wise woman foretold that where the spur struck, so would his head. The story goes that when brought back from the field, his skull was indeed smashed against the stone.

Office of Ordnance was located in the Tower, a central repository for royal guns and other ballistic weapons. Perhaps significant for the numbers of guns present, neither the eye-witness Salazar, who provided information for Diego de Valera, nor indeed Vergil, mention the use of cannon. *The Ballad of Bosworth Field* survives only in a mid-17th-century copy, but appears to be based on a work compiled within living memory of the battle by a member of Stanley's retinue, probably an eye-witness. It provides the clearest details on cannon used, though it must be remembered that this account could have embroidered upon the original. Richard, we are told, had 140 serpentines chained together in a row, and a similar number of bombards that blew 'like blasts of thunder'. Given the notorious medieval talent for miscounting, the size of the ridge, and the silence of de Valera and Vergil, this number seems either to be a wild overstatement by the original author or else poetic license. However, that some cannon were used seems likely. Molinet says the artillery fired at Richmond.

Both commanders probably made some sort of rousing speech to their troops, or at least to their commanders. The earliest source is Hall's 1540 manuscript, which borrows heavily from Vergil and then adds substantial battle speeches, strongly suggesting that he made them up. That is not to say that they do not reflect the sort of words which may well have been spoken, although given Richard's necessary swiftness in marshalling his troops, there was probably little time for overlong speeches. Richard apparently mentioned his repentance at his seizure of the crown (though note that this is a Tudor source) and reminds his followers of the inexperience of this 'unknown Welshman', of his army of traitors, who will fly or else beg forgiveness on seeing the royal banner, of the French and Bretons who 'our noble progenitors and your valiant parents have them oftener vanquished and overcome in one month than they … imagined possible … in a whole year'.

Henry Tudor highlighted the justice of his cause in God's eyes, related the bloody deeds of the king they were about to fight and reminded his followers that they had lost lands to his adherents. They could not turn back, 'so that here we stand like sheep in a fold circumcepted and compassed between our enemies and our doubtful friends'. This day would end their labour and the smaller their force the greater glory there would be in victory.

The position of the Stanleys

The forces of Lord Thomas Stanley and Sir William Stanley amounted to perhaps 5,000–6,000 men. About 3,000 of these, according to Vergil, were under Sir William. The problem with the Stanleys, the pivotal question which affects the whole reconstruction of the battle, relates to their position, apparently midway between the two armies. There are three possibilities: that they were to the north-west; that they were on either side; or that they were to the south-east. We may perhaps dispense with the second possibility. The idea that the forces were divided, with Sir William Stanley to the north-west and Lord Stanley to the south-east, is first implied in the speech Hall puts into the mouth of Henry Tudor: 'before us be our enemies and, on either side of us such as I neither surely trust nor greatly believe … here we stand … compassed between our enemies and our doubtful friends.' There is no reference to the Stanleys by name, and we have already seen that the speech seems to be an invention of Hall, relying heavily as he does on Vergil. The first account to relate the story is that of William Hutton's *The Battle of Bosworth Field*, written in 1788; it was then used by John Nichols in his *History and Antiquities of the County of Leicester*.

The Duke of Norfolk's division strives to break the stubborn resistance of Oxford's troops while King Richard and his household watch from the crest of Ambion Hill behind. Norfolk, distinguishable from the heraldic tabard bearing his coat-of-arms and marked by his square banner, fights in the midst of his men. The long, swallow-tailed standard of the Earl of Oxford displays his badge of the blue

boar. Beneath it is the square banner of Sir John Savage, who led the left wing of Henry's forces. The variety of armour, from full plate to padded jacks, testifies to the different ranks of fighting men involved in the struggle. The man-at-arms on the extreme left foreground is protected by a brigandine. Much in evidence are the staff weapons popular for combat on foot.

If the two Stanleys remained together, on which side did they take position? Whatever else is certain, they declined to join up with the king and equally held back from siding openly with Henry Tudor. It has been thought that they drew up on the high ground around Near Coton, to the north-west of the field. Both the ballads state that they were on a hill, and Bosworth Field mentions Sir William as coming down a 'back' or possibly 'bank'. It has been said that Vergil and other chronicles imply this, but Vergil does not mention a hill in his original text, nor do the others. A hill, in any case, does not necessarily imply the one at Near Coton. It could be the rising ground south-east of the battlefield. In fact, the hill at Near Coton is a good way from the field, so far that it is difficult to see anything until the troops are down in the valley. At present, the visitor centre on the field has placed a replica of Stanley's standard to the north-west, but this may be wrong.

One argument for not placing the Stanleys to the south-east has been the presence of the marsh, but there are two points to be made here. First, no one can say definitely how far the marsh originally extended in width or breadth. Second, there is no reason why the Stanleys were not arrayed beyond the marsh, on the slopes rising towards Dadlington. Shakespeare actually mentions Lord Stanley as being to the south of Richard's forces. Other factors also need to be taken into consideration. De Valera's account mentions a 'Lord Tamerlant', who is placed on the left of the king's line. He then moves out and round, but turns on the king and fights him. No units appear from other sources to execute such a manoeuvre; one is therefore left wondering who 'Lord Tamerlant' could be. The most obvious choice is Thomas, Lord Stanley, whose brother actively turns on Richard during the battle. De Valera notes earlier that 'Tamerlant' had agreed to fight for Henry before the latter's entry into England. Moreover, the names 'Tamerlant' and 'Stanley' are reasonably close and could understandably become confused to a Spanish visitor to England. It has also been suggested that 'Tamerlant' is a contraction of 'Stanley' and 'Northumberland'. If a misunderstanding for 'Northumberland' alone, it does not follow other sources, which maintain he never struck a blow. Northumberland, far from swinging round in front of Richard's troops to oppose them, does not seem to have taken any active part in the battle, and withdrew from the field later in the day.

Another possible explanation for De Valera's comments may be the probable movements of the Stanleys. Henry Tudor had sent a message to Lord Stanley as his division was assembling midway between the two protagonists, inviting him to join the formation. Stanley's reply was that Henry should concentrate on organising his own men and he would be 'at hand' (Vergil) with his own men drawn up. Henry, like Richard, cannot have been too pleased by his step-father's refusal to commit absolutely the large number of troops under his command. He must have felt greatly uneasy at the prospect of thousands of men menacingly holding off.

A king rides out. This illustration from *Ricart's Kalendar* of 1478–9 supposedly represents William the Conqueror, but the armour gives an idea of how Richard may have looked as he rode out to battle. Note the crown round the sallet. Footsoldiers surround the king. (Bristol City Record Office).

White Moors, the probable campsite of Henry Tudor on the night of 21 August. The battlefield lies a mile beyond the present tree-line.

Stanley withdrew his main battle up to a hill, but *The Ballad of Bosworth Field* suggests he sent a small select force to assist Henry. *Lady Bessy* mentions the troops under John Savage and Rhys ap Thomas. At about the same time Sir William Stanley seems to have moved closer to the invaders without actually coming alongside. Something of this may be sensed also in the account of Robert Lindsay, writing in the 1570s but drawing on oral tradition, when he notes that the royal vanguard which should have protected the king 'turned around and faced King Richard'.

These treacherous movements infuriated Richard, watching from Ambion Hill; his worst fears concerning the Stanleys were being realised and, in a rage, he gave orders that George Stanley, Lord Strange, be executed immediately. The ballads describe him bidding farewell to his kinsmen, friends and country, and telling his servant to take a ring to his wife, instructing her to flee with their child from England, so that he might one day be avenged. According to the Crowland chronicler, some councillors, worried about the outcome of the battle, persuaded Richard to postpone the execution; *Lady Bessy* relates how Sir William Harrington suggested Richard wait until all three Stanleys were taken, but to no avail. Either because of the confusion or else because those bearing the instructions had a mind to their future, the order was in fact never carried out.

The advance of Oxford

Henry Tudor's army must have been intimidated by the sight which greeted it. The crest of Ambion Hill was lined with soldiers and bristled

THE CLASH OF NORFOLK AND OXFORD, 22 AUGUST 1485

Richard gave orders that the enemy was to be attacked once they had passed the safety of the marsh. Oxford's men advanced, supported by Henry Tudor's forces.

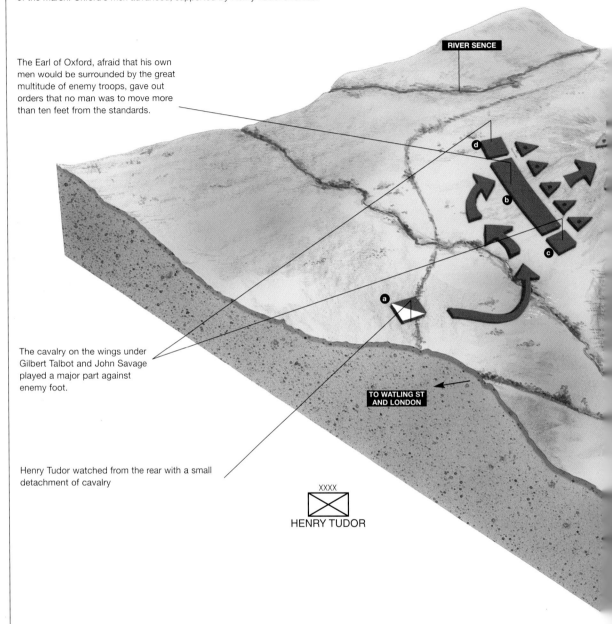

RIVER SENCE

The Earl of Oxford, afraid that his own men would be surrounded by the great multitude of enemy troops, gave out orders that no man was to move more than ten feet from the standards.

The cavalry on the wings under Gilbert Talbot and John Savage played a major part against enemy foot.

TO WATLING ST AND LONDON

Henry Tudor watched from the rear with a small detachment of cavalry

XXXX

HENRY TUDOR

REBELS		RICARDIANS	
a	Henry Tudor	1	Norfolk
b	Oxford	2	Richard III
c	Talbot	3	Northumberland
d	Savage	4	Ricardian Artillery

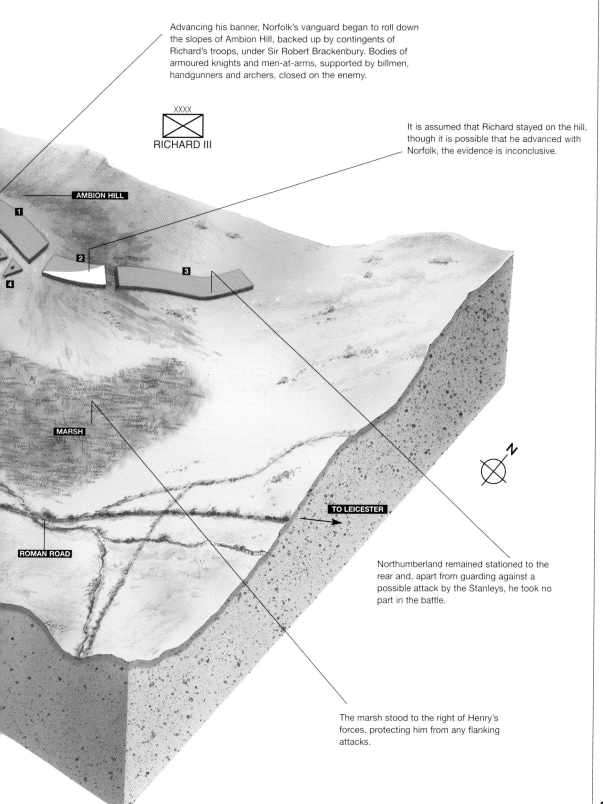

Advancing his banner, Norfolk's vanguard began to roll down the slopes of Ambion Hill, backed up by contingents of Richard's troops, under Sir Robert Brackenbury. Bodies of armoured knights and men-at-arms, supported by billmen, handgunners and archers, closed on the enemy.

XXXX

RICHARD III

It is assumed that Richard stayed on the hill, though it is possible that he advanced with Norfolk, the evidence is inconclusive.

AMBION HILL

1

2

3

4

MARSH

ROMAN ROAD

N

TO LEICESTER

Northumberland remained stationed to the rear and, apart from guarding against a possible attack by the Stanleys, he took no part in the battle.

The marsh stood to the right of Henry's forces, protecting him from any flanking attacks.

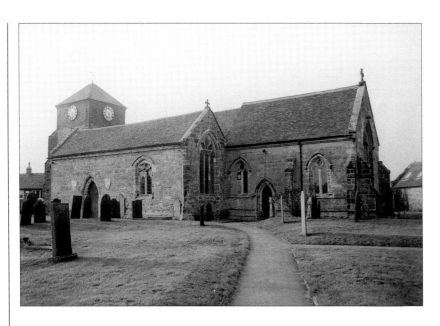

with weapons, but Henry's men did not stop. Under the command of the veteran Earl of Oxford, the main division continued to march purposefully forward. They crossed the Sence Brook and continued on towards the foot of Ambion Hill. Vergil notes that the marsh was on the right flank of the army, protecting the soldiers, while the sun was on their backs. Edward Hall caused confusion by adding that the sun was in the faces of Richard's troops, but this may be dismissed as a spurious comment. As Oxford's men moved slowly nearer, Richard ordered his gunners to open fire. Molinet describes how Henry's men were a quarter of a league away when the artillery began sending balls whistling into their ranks. He maintains that 'the French' then changed position and, instead of massing their troops against the main front of the royal line, aimed instead for the flank. There may have been a further reason for the initial movement directly towards Richard. It would have brought Oxford's division closer to the Stanleys and might have been partly done in the hope of stimulating these recalcitrant 'allies' to move forward to join the advancing body. Oxford may also had hoped to provoke the royalists into a cavalry charge which would bog down in the marsh. Either way, this aim was not realised. Of course, Oxford might simply have decided that a head-on attack against a long line sewn with cannon was liable to cause unacceptable casualties, and thus decided to risk marching his division parallel to the enemy until it was largely beyond the range of the royal cannon. This he did, until he faced the flank of

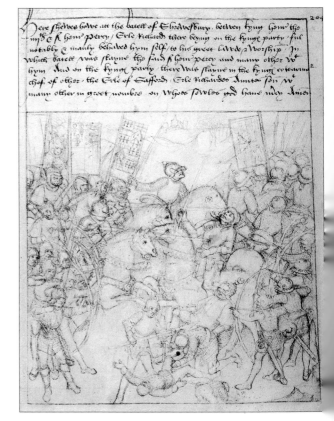

The spire of Market Bosworth church could be seen from the battlefield two miles to the south of the town.

Richard's line, where John Howard, Duke of Norfolk, waited for the signal to attack. If Henry also had some artillery, which may have been the case, it was probably obtained at Lichfield.

Richard gave orders that the enemy was to be attacked once they had passed the safety of the marsh. As Oxford's men came across and positioned themselves opposite Norfolk, the latter signalled to his archers in the front ranks of the vanguard. The formidable bowmen who had proved so effective against the French during the Hundred Years War were, during the Wars of the Roses, directed against each other. With a great shout, the archers drew back their strings and as the dreadful hail of arrows fell on Oxford's men, his own archers replied vigorously, sending their lethal bodkin-headed shafts whirring into Norfolk's men. Handgunners on both sides also opened fire. Norfolk must have been surprised by the bold response of the enemy and probably admired their spirit, but he could not let them draw breath. Advancing his banner, the entire vanguard began to roll down the slopes of Ambion Hill, backed up by contingents of Richard's troops, under Sir Robert Brackenbury. Bodies of armoured knights and men-at-arms, supported by billmen, handgunners and archers, closed on the enemy. The two divisions met somewhere at the foot of the hill. Now began the close combat butchery dealt out by swords, maces, axes and various staff weapons.

Richard, watching from the top of Ambion Hill, saw the collision of the two divisions and must have been frustrated to note that, far from fleeing or being pushed back, Oxford's men were standing their ground. The cavalry on the wings under Gilbert Talbot and John Savage would no doubt have played a major part against enemy foot. Vergil tells us that the Earl of Oxford, afraid that his own men would be surrounded by the great multitude of enemy troops, gave out orders that no man was to move more than ten feet from the standards. As a result, his troops tended to draw back and press together. Wary of a trap, Norfolk's line, too, drew back for a moment. Vergil adds that many men within the latter's division were relieved at this, not having any great heart to fight for Richard. To the king, still on Ambion Hill, this lacklustre performance and subsequent abatement of hostilities must have been worrying, and it is probable that thoughts of treachery were in his mind. Oxford, on the other hand, renewed the fighting. Vergil states that, while the earl battled on, others 'in the other part' advanced in 'facto cuneo'. This can be translated either as a wedge formation or else as a column. Either way, as Peter Foss points out, the tactic is a classic Roman military manoeuvre as laid down in the manuals of writers such as Vegetius. The narrow

The last charge of Richard III. In an effort to destroy Henry Tudor, Richard determined to reach him personally. De Valera says the king donned his coat-of-arms, which could mean either a heraldic tabard bearing the royal arms, or else a shield, still sometimes carried by mounted knights to help protect them from the initial shock from an enemy lance. He then put on his helmet with the gold circlet and left his position on Ambion Hill, leading his household retainers down the slope, thundering towards Henry's men with levelled lances. Here Richard crashed into his standard bearer, William Brandon, who was killed. Despite his lack of military training, Henry refused to flee in the face of this violent assault. As a furious mêlée developed, the bodyguards of both leaders closed together in a desperate struggle. Sir William Stanley's troops may have already been arriving to support Henry, and Richard realised that his bid had failed.

frontage was designed to push into an enemy formation and split the soldiers apart from one another, effectively breaking up the line. At long distance such a formation was more vulnerable to arrows since it had no line of archers to answer with, but at close range it could prove lethal. Since Vergil is careful to show that Oxford's main body fought on in line as before, it was presumably contingents under leaders such as Savage and Talbot that carried out this manoeuvre. *Lady Bessy* attributes the breaking of the royal line to Rhys ap Thomas.

The last charge

It was obvious that, as far as Richard was concerned, the battle was not going to plan. The enemy was not dispersed and was actually fighting well. It was Norfolk's men who seemed more likely to break. Indeed, some may already have started to drift away from the fighting. On the flank, Lord Stanley sat unmoving with a dangerously large body of men. Richard was then informed by spies that Henry Tudor was advancing. He strained his eyes until at last he recognised the other by his standards, floating on invisible staffs.

It has often been supposed that Henry had decided to ride across to Lord Stanley personally in order to persuade him to bring his men into the battle and relieve the hard-pressed division under the Earl of Oxford. None of the chroniclers or ballads describe this. What is certain is that Richard made a decision that would be momentous. Seeing the lacklustre performances by some of his soldiers and some desertions (by northerners, notes the Crowland chronicler) several of his men suggested that he flee. A swift horse, presumably preferable to the powerful but slower warhorse, was brought to him but he declined it. Salazar is described as openly counselling this course of action. Richard, well aware of the treason around him, nevertheless refused. 'Salazar, God forbid I yield one step. This day I will die as a king or win'.

He placed on his head the helmet encircled with the gold diadem. Shakespeare mentions that Richard rode 'White Surrey' that day, though this is unsubstantiated. Accompanied by his banner-bearer, Sir Percival Thirlwall, he gathered his close companions about him. These included Sir Robert Percy, controller of the household, and knights of the body such as Sir Ralph Ashton, Sir Thomas Broughton, Sir Marmaduke

Ambion Hill, looking down from the crest towards the probable position of Henry Tudor's army, now marked by the line of trees.

A reproduction of the standard of Richard III, floating on the top of Ambion Hill.

Constable, Sir John Grey, Sir James Harrington, Sir Thomas Markenfield, Sir John Neville, Sir Thomas Pilkington and Sir Richard Radcliffe. With a force of about 800 mounted men, he spurred down the slopes of Ambion Hill.

Some have seen this gallant charge as rather foolhardy. It is almost as if Richard had a death wish, echoed by the terrible dreams the night before. Yet his action was not really so rash or ill conceived. Richard knew he had to force the battle. He was well aware of the treachery in his army: the fact that Norfolk's division had failed to break Oxford, despite the loyalty of Norfolk himself; the reluctance of Northumberland to commit any of his men to the action; the Stanleys still watching the battle from a distance. Now he saw his main foe, the raw rival who dared challenge him in the field. Here was a chance to destroy Henry, or at the very least smash his guard and send him packing, then the whole of the invading force would crumble. Richard knew he must win the battle. He simply could not afford a stalemate, in which he might withdraw to fight another day. So obvious was the lack of support for him, that another day would, in all likelihood, see Henry with the greatest force. Richard had said at the outset that he must win or die in the attempt. The invaders had to be completely crushed.

Richard thundered down the south-west slopes on to the plain below, heading straight for Henry Tudor. His royal standard-bearer with him, his courageous charge – 'the swan-song of medieval English chivalry' as it has been called – must have been exhilarating, and meant action at last for the soldier king. He may well have roared his motto 'Loyaulte me lie!' to rally both himself and his followers. Aiming for the standard of Henry Tudor, he closed on the enemy ranks; the destriers reached the gallop and the lances came down. So powerful was this onslaught that Richard was borne into the thick of the press. His lance transfixed Henry's own standard-bearer, William Brandon, and the standard fell to the earth. The king's path was barred by the formidable Sir John Cheney; seizing

THE DEATH OF KING RICHARD, 22 AUGUST 1485

Oxford's men fend off the assault by Norfolk's troops, Norfolk himself is slain in combat. Seeing the standards of Henry Tudor across the field the king tries to destroy him and bring a swift end to the battle.

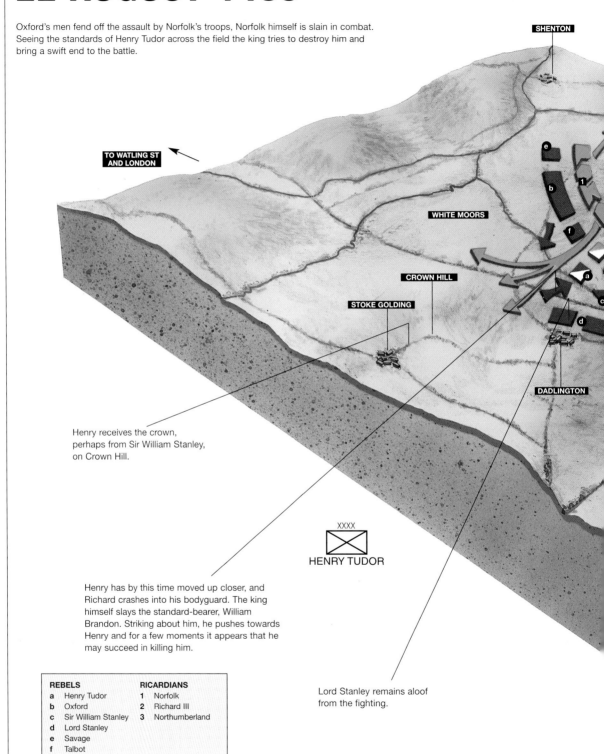

SHENTON

TO WATLING ST AND LONDON

WHITE MOORS

CROWN HILL

STOKE GOLDING

DADLINGTON

Henry receives the crown, perhaps from Sir William Stanley, on Crown Hill.

XXXX
HENRY TUDOR

Henry has by this time moved up closer, and Richard crashes into his bodyguard. The king himself slays the standard-bearer, William Brandon. Striking about him, he pushes towards Henry and for a few moments it appears that he may succeed in killing him.

Lord Stanley remains aloof from the fighting.

REBELS		RICARDIANS	
a	Henry Tudor	1	Norfolk
b	Oxford	2	Richard III
c	Sir William Stanley	3	Northumberland
d	Lord Stanley		
e	Savage		
f	Talbot		

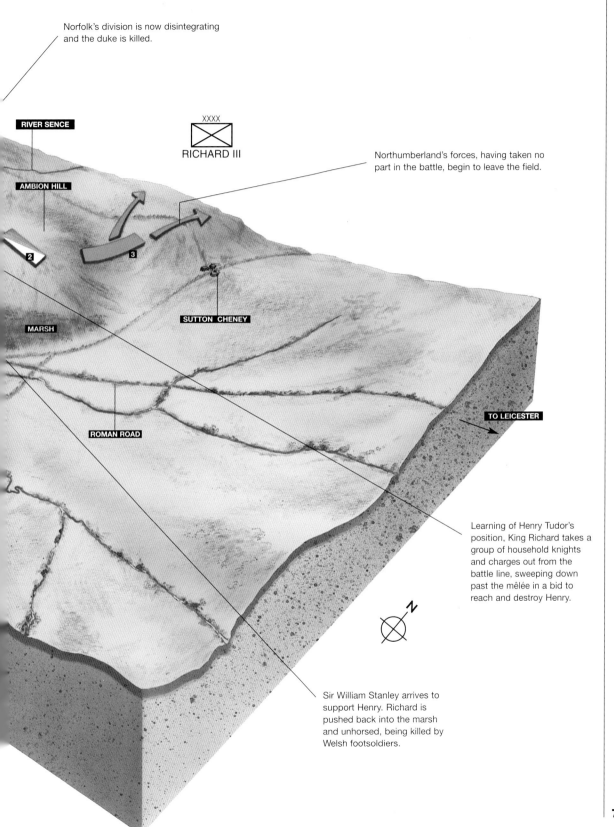

Norfolk's division is now disintegrating and the duke is killed.

RIVER SENCE

XXXX

RICHARD III

Northumberland's forces, having taken no part in the battle, begin to leave the field.

AMBION HILL

2

3

SUTTON CHENEY

MARSH

TO LEICESTER

ROMAN ROAD

N

Learning of Henry Tudor's position, King Richard takes a group of household knights and charges out from the battle line, sweeping down past the mêlée in a bid to reach and destroy Henry.

Sir William Stanley arrives to support Henry. Richard is pushed back into the marsh and unhorsed, being killed by Welsh footsoldiers.

an axe, war hammer or possibly a mace, Richard beat him out of the saddle. He looked about him for his main target, the 'Welsh milksop'.

Henry, to his soldiers' probable surprise and relief, showed admirable courage and refused to give up his position. Heartened by his stand, his bodyguard fought on vigorously and denied Richard a path to their master. His chance of destroying Henry and ending the battle at a single stroke was ebbing away. As he strove to reach him, Richard was brought to a near standstill and was gradually pushed back. Things were starting to go horribly wrong. The powerful Rhys Fawr ap Maredudd had taken up Henry's dragon standard and defended it manfully. Richard's own standard-bearer, Sir Percival Thirlwall, was already unhorsed and had both legs hewn off, probably by a hand-and-a-half sword or else a staff weapon. Heroically, he clung to the standard and refused to let it fall. Shakespeare makes Richard say: 'I think there be six Richmonds in the field; five have I slain today instead of him.' This interesting comment reflects a practice occasionally employed in which decoys were dressed in identical garb to the commander. Whether there is any truth in such a statement with regard to Bosworth is speculative; no other writer mentions any decoys.

The death of King Richard

And now, at last, the Stanleys showed their hand. Into the mêlée came Sir William Stanley with his red-coated followers. Sweeping across they came to the aid of the beleaguered Henry Tudor and swirled around the embattled King Richard. Whatever people thought of him, all chroniclers respected the courage Richard showed in the face of now hopeless odds.

King Richard's Well, or King Dick's Well, on the southern slope of Ambion Hill. Tradition has it that Richard drank from this spring during the battle, though it is most likely that, if he drank from it at all, it was in the early morning when he missed breakfast. The cairn was raised over the spot in the 19th century and restored in 1964. It should be noted that there is more than one spring in the area.

'But yet, if I may say the truth to his credit, though small in body and feeble of limb, he bore himself like a gallant knight and acted with distinction as his own champion until his last breath, shouting oftentimes that he was betrayed, and crying "Treason! Treason! Treason!"' So said John Rous of Warwick, in about 1490, a writer at first complimentary to Richard's rule, but later a great Tudor supporter. Richard's heroic charge had run its course and Henry still lived. Around him his loyal knights were being killed, and the king must have known that his cause was lost. Few chronicles give many details of his last minutes, but John Molinet mentions that Richard's horse jumped into a marsh and got bogged down. This gives further credence to the view that Richard's charge was down the south-eastern slopes of Ambion Hill, and that, once down on the level ground – Redmore Plain – he was driven back into the marshy ground or wetlands. Molinet further reveals that a Welshman then slew him with a halberd. This fits with the idea that Sir William Stanley's infantry, which contained many Welshmen, were closing in and were indeed coming across the southern side of the battlefield. They may well have been formed up behind Henry. Whether or not Richard was killed by a blow from a halberd, once down, his body was mutilated. The story fits well with an 18th-century tradition known in the area, while a Welsh tradition credits Rhys ap Thomas with killing the king; Rhys Fawr ap Maredudd also claimed that he killed the king. The English sources are so bare on fact that it is almost certain that Richard was killed by footsoldiers; if knights or nobles had been involved it would have been made public knowledge. How far across the plain the final struggle took place is, again, conjecture. Part of the problem lies in the extent of the marshy ground. It is possible that Richard died on the fringes of what is now Ambion Wood. Alternatively, he may have swept by the edges of the marsh, if Henry was well to the rear, eventually becoming bogged down in the wetlands further south. A proclamation by Henry shortly after the battle mentions the place of Richard's death as 'Sandeford', a name which no longer exists. Foss suggests it refers to a crossing of Fenn Lanes over the wetlands north of Stoke Golding. The idea that Richard rode north-west is based on Sandeford being the place where the sand road, used by villagers from Sutton Cheney and Shenton to extract sand and gravel, crossed a stream – 'King Richard's Field'. It may well be, however, that 'Sandeford' simply refers to the battle generally.

Norfolk, too, lay slain; *The Song of Lady Bessy* says it was Sir John Savage who cornered him near a windmill. On the other hand, Molinet asserts that Norfolk was captured and brought to Oxford, who had him executed. Certainly Oxford had good reason to hate Norfolk, who had taken his lands. They had been ranged against each other at the battle of Barnet in 1471, where Oxford had gained the upper hand before the

A pottery drinking costrel said to have been found on the battlefield. (Leicester Museums)

Yorkists took the field. Now things were
different. According to tradition, the Earl of
Surrey defended himself well until captured.

The battle was effectively over about two hours after
it had begun. With their king dead, the army began to
melt away. Northumberland left Ambion Hill without striking
a blow. Others laid down their weapons and made off; there was
no point fighting for a lost cause. Oxford's men, however, having
put their enemies to flight, cut them down in the rout which followed.
This is generally supposed to have been south-westwards, towards
Dadlington and Stoke Golding, since armour, weapons and bones were
turned up, likely signs of the carnage that followed a rout. It has been suggested
that the whole battle was in this area. However, skeletons from the battle of
Towton were discovered a mile from the area in which the main battle took place,
the me presumably killed in the rout. As men streamed away, Henry Tudor
looked on the field of which he was the victor.

King Richard faces death. Forced away from Henry Tudor by the press of men, he is pushed back into the marshy ground, where he finds himself surrounded by enemy troops. Many of these are retainers of Sir William Stanley, who has now entered the battle. Some of his men are distinguishable by their red livery and badge of a silver hart's head. The king's horse, stuck in the boggy ground, is dying from its wounds, while his standard-bearer, Sir Percival Thirlwall, gallantly holds up the standard despite losing both legs. Richard holds a war hammer, designed for crushing armour and more likely than the battle axe of the ballads. According to Molinet, the king was felled by a halberd wielded by a Welshman. All the chroniclers agree that Richard died fighting bravely.

AFTERMATH

The king is dead, long live the king. Richard III may have died valiantly, but he was destined to be vilified at the hands of the victors. His mangled corpse, besmirched with mud and blood, was stripped naked and slung over a horse. Meanwhile, Henry Tudor removed to a nearby hill near the village of Stoke Golding, to a place which became known as Crown Hill (first mentioned in records of 1605). Here he received Richard's crown, which, according to both the Croyland chronicler and Vergil, was found among the spoils. Later legend has it that it was found in a thorn bush. There is no mention of this in any of the 15th-century or Tudor sources, not even in Shakespeare, though it would have made a good story. However, it is difficult otherwise to explain why the hawthorn became so prominent in Tudor iconography, appearing, among other places, on the tomb of Henry VII. The crown was received from Stanley, but exactly which one is also difficult to prove. Vergil and the ballads relate that it was Lord Stanley, yet on 16 January 1486, the latter swore an oath to a papal commission that he had not known his stepson until two days after the battle (though he may have met him the previous day). It is possible that it was Sir William who brought the crown, perhaps handed it by Reginald Bray. Since Sir William fell from grace in 1495, accused of treason, it would not do for a chronicler to remind his audience that King Henry had received his crown from a traitor twice over. The more contemporary *Great Chronicle of London* suggests Sir William passed it to Henry almost without thinking. However, Professor Chrimes does point out that, even if it was Sir William who brought the crown, it would be

The view from the crest, looking north-eastwards towards Northumberland's position (right) in the rear of Richard's host.

A gold seal ring, its bezel bearing the emblem of an enamelled boar. Believed to have been found at Bosworth, the ring is of late 15th-century date and may have been dropped by a Ricardian supporter. (By permission of His Grace the Duke of Devonshire)

odd if he had not then handed it to his elder brother, the only peer not attainted, to place it on Henry's head.

Richard's corpse, carried behind a pursuivant called Norrey, according to the *Great Chronicle* (not Blanc Sent Leger as John Speed later asserts), was then taken back to Leicester. For two days the body, naked but for a piece of cloth for decency, was displayed in the Church of St Mary of the Annunciation in the Newarke, for all to see that Richard was truly dead. It was then put in a plain tomb, without stone or epitaph, in the house of the Grey Friars, near St Martin's. Ten years later Henry VII paid the paltry sum of £10 1s. to provide a tomb, an alabaster monument was placed over it, carved by Walter Hylton of Nottingham. Grey Friars was dissolved at the Reformation, the king's bones were thrown into the River Soar and the royal tomb was taken and used as a horse-trough outside the White Horse Inn. By 1758 it had been broken up and used as part of the inn's cellar steps; even this has now gone. Professor Ross has pointed out that apart from the unusual case of the boy king, Edward V, Richard III is the only English king since 1066 not to have an accredited and splendid tomb.

Among Richard's forces, casualties were heavy, notably among the king's closest circle. The Duke of Norfolk, Lord Ferrers of Chartley, Sir Robert Brackenbury, Sir Richard Ratcliffe, Sir Robert Percy and John Kendall, the king's secretary, were all killed in the battle. Sir William Catesby fled, but was caught and executed in Leicester two days later. The Earls of Surrey and Northumberland were taken into custody, probably in the Tower. The Earl of Lincoln, Viscount Lovell, and Humphrey and Thomas Stafford all escaped. Vergil reports that 1,000 were slain, which may be an overstatement, and that Henry lost only 100, which is probably an understatement. The only notable casualty on Henry Tudor's side was William Brandon. Reports coming from the field testify to the confusion as to who had been killed. Even Henry was not certain, ordering the arrest of Sir Richard Ratcliffe five days after his death in the battle.

Henry repaired to Leicester. One story relates how the keeper of the White Boar Inn displayed his allegiance to Oxford by hurriedly repainting the sign blue! Henry sent Robert Willoughby to Sheriff Hutton in Yorkshire to secure the person of Edward, Earl of Warwick, the 15-year-old son of George, Duke of Clarence, and a potential threat. He was brought down to London and placed in the Tower, where he remained for the rest of his life. Elizabeth of York was brought from the same fortress to be reunited with her mother, Queen Elizabeth Woodville. Within days of the battle Henry sent out a circular letter telling of the battle in which 'Richard, Duke of Gloucester, lately called King Richard, was slain at a place called Sandeford, within the shire of Leicester'. The letter must have been hurriedly composed, since it mentions Thomas, Earl of Surrey, among the slain, when he had in fact survived. It also commands, on pain of death, that no man interfere with the 'commons' who were fleeing from the field, nor that anyone rob or pillage or pick old or new quarrels.

By 3 September, Henry, splendidly arrayed, was received at Shoreditch by the city representatives with trumpets blowing. Stopping at St Pauls, Henry deposited three flags, presumably those used at Bosworth – one with the arms of St George, one with a red dragon on white and green sarcenet, and one of Tarteron and Duncow. After prayers and a Te Deum, Henry withdrew to the palace of the Bishop of London, where he stayed for a few days.

In the next three or four months Henry set about rewarding his followers. His uncle, Jasper Tudor, won the biggest gift, being created Duke of Bedford; he would marry Catherine Woodville, sister to Edward IV's queen and widow of Henry Stafford, Duke of Buckingham. He was also appointed chief justice of South Wales, and given numerous other rewards. John de Vere, Earl of Oxford, was restored to his titles lost under the Yorkists, and created admiral of England, Ireland and Aquitaine, and then constable of the Tower of London and keeper of the lions and leopards, with the usual fees. Thomas, Lord Stanley, became Earl of Derby, then constable of England, chief steward of the duchy of Lancaster and received other manors. His wife and Henry's mother, Margaret Beaufort, was restored to her lands and given other rewards. Sir William Stanley became chamberlain of the royal household, a chamberlain of the exchequer, and latterly constable of Caernarfon Castle and chief justice of North Wales, and was given other lands. As well as rewards for many others in the campaign, Henry did not forget more humble servants who supported him both in Brittany and France; upwards of 40 (mostly of yeoman rank) received gifts from the grateful monarch.

On 25 September 1485, Henry ordered commissions of array to be sent to the Border counties to counter any threat from a possible Scots invasion. Whether James III had sent a contingent to assist Henry's bid for the throne cannot be proved (no English chronicler mentions it), and there was no good reason to expect an attack. In the event nothing materialised and things seemed set fair for a friendly relationship with Scotland.

On Sunday 30 October 1485, Henry Tudor was anointed and crowned as King Henry VII.

Henry attainted Richard III and 28 others for treason; his reign would see 138 persons attainted, with only 52 reversed, while Richard had attainted 100 in two years but

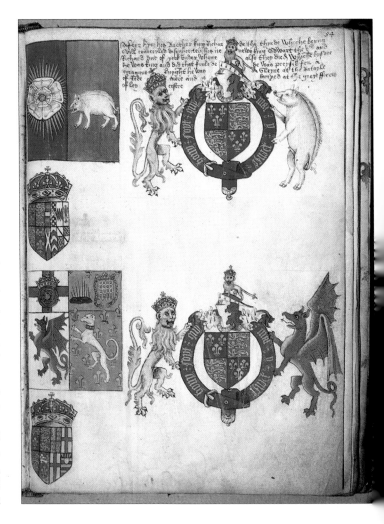

Prince Arthur's Book, **compiled before 1519, depicts the royal arms of Richard III. To the left are the badges of the white rose en soleil and the white boar on livery colours of blue and murray with (below) his arms impaled with those of his wife, Anne Neville. At bottom are the royal arms of Henry VII. His badges of the red dragon, greyhound, Tudor rose, sunburst and portcullis on livery colours white and green are shown left with (below) his arms impaled with those of his queen, Elizabeth of York. (College of Arms, Vincent MS. 152 p.54)**

INSURRECTIONS AGAINST HENRY VII, 1487–1497

Legend:
- Earl of Lincoln with Lambert Simnel
- Henry VII
- Perkin Warbeck
- Henrician supporters
- Cornish rebels

0   50   100 Miles
0   50   100   150 Km

SCOTLAND

Warbeck at Stirling
20 November 1495

Forth Stirling

Edinburgh

Berwick-upon-Tweed

Scots invasion of England
17 September 1496

Clyde

Ayr

Tweed

Warbeck leaves Ayr
before 6 July 1497

Latimer

NORTH
SEA

Newcastle
upon Tyne

*Lough
Foyle*

Donegal

Carlisle

Eden

P e n n i n e s

Masham
8 June 1487

1497

Barrow
4 June 1487

Masham

Northumberland

Possible route to
Scotland 1495

IRELAND

Shannon

IRISH
SEA

Barrow

Clifford

York

Ouse

**Warbeck
from
Vlissingen**

Galway

Barrow

Dublin

**Earl of Lincoln
with Simnel**

Nottingham
14 June 1487

Aire

✗ Bramham Moor
10 or 11 June 1487

Doncaster

✗ East Stoke
16 June 1487

23 July - 3 August
joins siege of
Waterford

Dee

Stanleys

Newark

Radcliffe
Loughborough

Trent

Nottingham

✗ East Stoke

King's Lynn

Tralee

Blackwater

Youghal

Waterford

Stafford

Derby

Leicester

Norwich

Nene

Gt. Ouse

EAST
ANGLIA

Great
Yarmouth

Cork

Ardmore

Shrewsbury

Severn

Coventry

Cambridge

Kinsale

Warbeck raids
Youghal

Wye

Henry VII

Woodstock

Cork
26 July 1497

1497

Oxford

Landing near Deal
3 July 1495

Daubney

Bristol

Bath

Thames

London

Deal

Minehead

Wells

Salisbury

Guildford

Skirmish at
Guildford

KENT

Rye

Calais

Warbeck lands at
Whitesand Bay
7 September 1497

Exeter
17 -18 September
1497

Taunton

Taunton
19 - 20
September

Southampton

✗

**Willoughby
de Broke**

Portsmouth

Bodmin

Exeter

CORNWALL

Daubney

Reading

✗ Blackheath
Cornishmen routed
17 June 1497

Lands End

Penzance

Plymouth

1495

ENGLISH CHANNEL

✗ Warbeck surrenders
at Beaulieu Abbey
5 October 1497

WALES

ENGLAND

NORTHUMBERLAND

reversed all but one. An oath was exacted at the first parliament from the knights and squires of the king's household, the men of the house of Commons, and the lords temporal and spiritual. On 18 January 1486 Henry married Elizabeth of York. His progeny would now represent the united houses of Lancaster and York. The badge of the Tudor rose, which incorporated the white rose of York with the red rose of Lancaster, was to be used prolifically by the Tudors.

The view from Ambion Hill looking towards Dadlington in the distance (left, beyond the present tree-line), the possible location of one or both Stanleys. Stoke Golding is in the centre distance.

Plots and Pretenders

In April 1486, while at Lincoln, Henry received word that a plot was being fomented against him. Francis, Viscount Lovell, together with Humphrey and Thomas Stafford, had been in sanctuary at Colchester since the defeat at Bosworth. Now they broke their sanctuary and set about raising revolt. Lovell headed north into Yorkshire while the Staffords went into Worcestershire. Henry did not know just how deep this insurrection might prove to be, or how many Yorkist sympathisers might crawl out of the woodwork. As it turned out the whole affair collapsed without much ado. Lovell escaped into Lancashire and took ship for Flanders but the Staffords were both captured, being dragged from sanctuary; Humphrey was executed, but his younger brother was pardoned.

Although this insurrection had caused little problem, there followed in 1487 a more serious threat. Edward IV's father, Richard, Duke of York, had been king's lieutenant in Ireland during the reign of Henry VI, and had used his time to build up a strong advocacy for the Yorkist cause in Ireland. As Earl of March and Ulster, Lord of Trim and Connacht, he could be seen as at least partly Irish, and was supported by the Anglo-Irish lords. When he arrived in July 1449 with the black dragon standard of Ulster carried before him, he had received a warm welcome. On 21 October his son, George (later Duke of Clarence), was born in Dublin Castle. The Irish lords who wished for home rule used York's parliament at Drogheda to declare the legislative and legal independence of Ireland. The most powerful rulers for a while were the Earls of Kildare.

After Henry VII came to the throne it was obvious to the earls and those lords who supported home rule that Ireland could not be ruled in the name of the Yorkist regime, and that either they embrace the new regime or actively try to topple it. When Lambert Simnel was brought to Dublin, they chose the latter course. Simnel, the ten-year-old son of an Oxford joiner, had been trained to impersonate Edward, Earl of Warwick, who was in fact securely immured in the Tower. As the son of the Duke of Clarence, Warwick was a Yorkist figurehead, and having been born in Dublin he was even more attractive to the Irish lords. Hardly anyone was fooled by the deception, but Simnel was a useful tool and a potent figurehead under his pseudonym. John, Earl of Lincoln, himself the son of Edward IV's sister, Elizabeth, now showed his hand and fled to Flanders to join Lovell. Margaret of Burgundy provided them with money and 2,000 German mercenaries under the formidable commander, Martin Schwartz. Their arrival in Dublin on 5 May encouraged the Yorkists and the coronation of Simnel as Edward VI took place on 24 May. Together with some Irish troops, they took ship and landed at Barrow on 4 June. Marching inland, they crossed into Yorkshire and, at Bramham Moor near York on 10 or 11 June, drove off troops of the Earl of Northumberland and Sir Robert Clifford. They marched on south, crossing the Trent. The defection of Lincoln had driven home to Henry the seriousness of the situation. He had ordered the west coast to be guarded, and moved up to Kenilworth on 8 May. From there he advanced to Nottingham, where the Stanleys joined him on 14 June. On learning the whereabouts of the enemy force, the royal army moved towards Newark, and on 16 June encountered the rebels near East Stoke. There is little information about the battle apart from that provided by Polydore Vergil 30 years later. The rebels had the River Trent on their right flank. The Germans fought fiercely, as did the Irish, but the latter's lack of body armour resulted in heavy casualties. Only the first line of the royal forces appears to have been engaged and it is not stated why the others did not take part, given that a long indecisive struggle took place.

If the Stanleys were to the north, then Sir William may have waited in the middle distance, now marked by a modern standard. Some believe that Lord Stanley was also on this side, in which case he would be well to the rear.

Some of the contingents from Henry's centre may have joined the battle late. However, eventually a final charge was enough to break the rebel ranks. Viscount Lovell seems to have fled and disappears from history. The Earl of Lincoln, Martin Schwartz and the Irish leader were among those killed. Simnel was captured but was not executed. He was set to work in the royal kitchens and eventually became king's falconer. His teacher, a priest called Richard Simons, was imprisoned for life.

The battle of Stoke was the final battle in the Wars of the Roses, yet only four years later a second pretender appeared in Cork. Perkin Warbeck was a Frenchman who claimed to be Richard of York, the young prince who disappeared in the Tower. This was a much more difficult threat to counter. Henry sent a small force to Ireland, but Warbeck obtained little Irish support, and was received instead at the court of Charles VIII of France. Henry secured a treaty with France and Brittany which also specified that Warbeck should receive no support, so the pretender moved on and was welcomed by Margaret of Burgundy and by Archdukes Philip and Maximilian. Henry broke off trade with Flanders and set in train attainders, the most important of which was that of Sir William Stanley. Found to be in league with Warbeck, Stanley was beheaded in February 1495. Warbeck, given a small expeditionary force by Margaret of Burgundy and Maximilian, appeared off the coast of Kent and landed some troops near Deal on 3 July. With Stanley dead, the plot had no real chance and the invaders received no support. Seeing his men killed or captured, Warbeck left them to their fate and sailed on to Ireland. An attack by his sympathisers on Waterford was resisted until relieved by Sir Edward Poynings from Dublin. Warbeck then moved to Scotland, where James IV entertained him, despite a truce with Henry VII. Receiving limited assistance from Margaret, the invasion of England by 'Richard IV' finally began on 17 September 1496. James grew suspicious when Warbeck received no support. The countryside was devastated and the horrified Warbeck turned back, leaving James to seize a few watchtowers before he too retreated in the face of an English force under Lord Latimer. James agreed to terms with Henry, and Warbeck, bereft of his ally, left Scotland and went via Ireland to Cornwall, arriving at Lands End on 7 September 1497. An insurrection perhaps largely against taxation had been defeated at Blackheath on 17 June but gave him some hope of support from this quarter. With only a few thousand local men, he was rebuffed by Exeter and Taunton and then confounded by a pincer movement of swiftly mobilised royal troops to north and south. After surrendering at Beaulieu Abbey on 5 October he was treated well, but then unwisely tried to flee and was put in the Tower, where he was later convicted of conspiring with Edward of Warwick. Warbeck was hanged on 16 November 1499 and Warwick was finally beheaded on Tower Hill 13 days later. So ended the last Yorkist threat to Tudor rule. There would be other threats, but Henry VII would survive, amassing great wealth, until he left his throne to his formidable surviving son, Henry VIII, in 1509.

The position of Oxford's division as it passed the marsh and came into range of Norfolk's archers. The hilltop above would have been crammed with men and bristling with weapons. It was around here that the main fighting probably took place.

A modern replica of Henry Tudor's standard, seen from the slopes of Ambion Hill, may mark the area where Norfolk and Oxford clashed.

Market Bosworth is a small town some eight miles west of Leicester and the M1, and about six miles north-east of Atherstone and the A5. The battlefield itself lies some two miles south of Market Bosworth, and is well signposted. It can be reached most directly by turning off the A447 and driving through Sutton Cheney. The church here has many memories of Richard in the form of white boar badges, inscriptions etc., though solid proof that he actually worshipped here is, sadly, wanting. A right turn by the church, again signposted, leads down the road to the track up to the visitor centre and car park on Ambion Hill. The centre is well worth a visit. There is an exhibition area which includes models of the battle and of the soldiers, illustrations, contemporary accounts, and examples of period weapons and armour, though battlefield relics have largely been relegated to the 17th-century Civil War skirmish. A small cinema shows the battle scene from Laurence Olivier's Richard III, which at least gives an impression of events, though strictly speaking is of dubious value. A well-stocked shop, refreshment area and conveniences are provided.

The battlefield has changed greatly from its original appearance. The marsh was drained in the late 16th century and the land enclosed in the 17th century when Ambion Wood was planted. The Ashby-de-la-Zouche canal cuts through Henry Tudor's line of advance from White Moors, as does a Victorian railway line (now the Battlefield Line and another means of reaching the site).

From the grassy top of the car park and picnic area, a path leads off to the right, to take in the main position of Richard's troops. A modern standard marks this place, and all along the visitor trail numbered viewpoint information panels guide the visitor. Passing down the north-eastern slope, Northumberland's position towards the rear is seen from the track. Also from this area is shown the controversial northern position of the Stanleys, again with a standard. At the bottom of the hill, Shenton railway station conveniently marks the rough position of Oxford's division. Marked by a modern copy of Henry's dragon standard, the path turns at the station to run parallel with the tracks and enters the edge of Ambion Wood. The marsh was probably somewhere in this vicinity. Moving round the hillside and up the south-eastern slope the path reaches King Dick's Well before climbing back to the car park. This walk gives a good brief tour round the main features of the site, but extended walks are also possible.

The memorial stone to the alleged site of Richard's death after riding down the north-west slopes is reached by rejoining the road from Sutton Cheney and continuing on towards Shenton. Turning left at the junction, the marker is in a field on the right (it can also be reached on foot from Shenton station). Continuing on, this road joins the Roman road which traversed the southern edges of the field; crossing over this will lead to Dadlington and to Stoke Golding; Crown Hill is immediately west of the village. White Moors can be reached by joining the Roman road towards Atherstone, then making a right turn off it towards Shenton. White Moors is now marked by a Tudor banner and has a car park and picnic area but the view towards Ambion Hill is masked by the woods. Rejoining the Roman road towards Atherstone, a right turn on to the A5 (Watling St) leads to the town. Almost beyond it, a left turn leads to the remains of Merevale Abbey.

The garter stall plate of Thomas, Lord Stanley. (Reproduced by permission of the Dean and Canons of Windsor)

This may be the view Henry Tudor had as Richard charged down the hill towards him.

1452	**2 October:** birth of Richard III in Fotheringhay Castle.
1457	**28 January:** birth of Henry Tudor in Pembroke Castle.
1461	**4 March:** accession of Edward IV.
	29 March: battle of Towton.
	1 November: Richard created Duke of Gloucester.
1470	**3 October:** readeption of Henry VI.
1471	**14 April:** battle of Barnet. Death of Warwick the 'Kingmaker'.
	4 May: battle of Tewkesbury.
	2 June: Jasper and Henry Tudor escape from Tenby.
1482	**July–August:** Scottish expedition by Richard of Gloucester.
1483	**9 April:** accession of Edward V.
	30 April: Edward V placed under protection of Richard of Gloucester
	26 June: accession of Richard III.
	11 October: Richard learns of revolt in southern England.
	12 October: Henry Tudor attempts landing from Brittany.
	2 November: execution of the Duke of Buckingham.
	25 December: oath of Henry Tudor at Rennes to marry Elizabeth of York.
1484	**25 January:** Henry attainted.
	9 April: death of Edward, Prince of Wales.
1485	**16 March:** death of Queen Anne.

Looking north from the northern boundaries of Ambion Wood up Ambion Hill. This section of the field may cover part of the marshy ground, which was drained in the 16th century. If so, this area may be on the western edges of the marsh, into which King Richard was finally pushed and surrounded by Stanley's men. His death may have occurred somewhere in this vicinity.

1 August: Henry Tudor sets sail from Harfleur.

7 August: Henry Tudor lands at Milford Haven.

11 August: Richard at Nottingham hears of the landing of Henry Tudor.

15 or 16 August: Henry reaches Shrewsbury.

20 August: Henry reaches Atherstone. Richard arrives in Leicester.

21 August: Henry camps at White Moors. Richard camps near Ambion Hill.

22 August: the battle of Bosworth. Richard III killed.

30 October: Henry Tudor crowned king.

The meadows by Fenn Lanes south-west of the Sence Brook with, in the distance, Dadlington on the left, Stoke Golding on the right and Crown Hill on the extreme right. Peter Foss, who believes the marsh was in this vicinity, suggests this as the area in which Richard perished.

1486   **18 January:** Henry VII marries Elizabeth of York.
      April: Plot by Lovell, Humphrey Stafford and Thomas Stafford.
1487   **24 May:** Coronation of Lambert Simnel as Edward VI in Dublin.
      4 June: Simnel lands at Barrow.
      10 or 11 June: Northumberland's troops driven off at Bramham Moor.
      16 June: battle of Stoke. Final battle in Wars of the Roses.
1491   **November:** Perkin Warbeck proclaimed as Richard, Duke of York.
1495   **16 February:** Sir William Stanley beheaded for treason.
      23 July–3 August: Warbeck's expedition appears off Kent but landing force routed.
1496   **17 September:** Warbeck marches from Scotland but invasion collapses.
1497   **17 June:** Cornish uprising beaten at Blackheath.
      7 September: Warbeck lands in Cornwall.
      5 October: Warbeck surrenders.
1499   **16 November:** execution of Warbeck.
      29 November: execution of Edward, Earl of Warwick.

Fenn Lanes, now a metalled road, looking westwards. The line of trees marks the brook around which Peter Foss believes lay the marsh. Whether the latter was this far south-west, and whether therefore Richard charged across here, is disputed. Almost certainly fleeing royalists passed across here during the rout from the main mêlée on the right.

FURTHER READING

If the Stanleys were arrayed to the north of the field, as some still think, then it is down this slope that Richard would have thundered in his final charge.

Bennett, Michael, *The Battle of Bosworth,* (2nd edn.), Stroud. 1993

Boardman, Andrew W., *The Medieval Soldier in the Wars of the Roses,* Stroud, 1998

Burne, Alfred H., *The Battlefields of England,* London, 1950

Chrimes, S. B., *Henry VII,* London, 1972

Foss, Peter, *The Field of Redemore: The Battle of Bosworth, 1485,* (2nd edn.) Newtown Linford, 1998

Gairdner, J., 'The Battle of Bosworth', *Archaeologia,* LV i, 1896 (reprinted with introduction and some extracts from contemporary accounts, Richard III Society, 1975)

Harris, O. D., '" … Even here, in Bosworth Field": a Disputed Site of Battle', *The Ricardian,* VII, no. 92, March 1986

Phillips, M. J., 'The Battle of Bosworth: Further Reflections on the Battlefield Site', *The Ricardian,* VII, no.96, March 1987

Richmond, Colin, 'The Battle of Bosworth', *History Today,* 35, August 1985

Ross, Charles, *Richard III,* London, 1981

Ross, Charles, *The Wars of the Roses,* London, 1976

Rowse, A. L., *Bosworth Field and the Wars of the Roses,* London, 1966

Williams, Daniel, '"A Place Mete for Twoo Battayles to Encountre": The Siting of the Battle of Bosworth, 1485', *The Ricardian,* VII, no. 90, Sept. 1985

Williams, D.T., *The Battle of Bosworth Field*, (new edn.), Leicester, 1996

Original Sources

Many sources relating to the battle itself are translated or transcribed in Bennett. For additional material see:

Commines, Philippe de, *Memoirs. The Reign of Louis XI, 1461–1483*, ed. Jones, M., London, 1972

Fabian, Robert, *The Great Chronicle of London*, ed. Thomas, A. H. and Thornley, I. D., London, 1938

Molinet, Jean, *Chroniques de Jean Molinet (1474–1506)*, ed. Doutrepont, G. and Jodogne, O., 3 vols, Brussels, 1935–7

Rous, John, *Historia Johannis Rossi Warwicensis de Regibus Anglie*, ed. Hearne, T., London, 1716

Valera, Diego de, 'A Spanish account of the battle of Bosworth', trans. Nokes, E. M. and Wheeler, G., *The Ricardian*, II, no. 36, 1972, p.2

Vergil, Polydore, *Three Books of Polydore Vergil's 'English History'*, comprising the Reigns of Henry VI, Edward IV and Richard III, from an Early Translation, preserved among the Manuscripts of the Old Royal Library in the British Museum, ed. Ellis, H., Camden Society old series 29, 1844, pp.221–6

The Ballad of Bosworth Field, Bishop Percy's Folio Manuscript. Ballads and Romances, ed. Hales, J. W. and Furnivall, F. J., 3 vols, London, 1868, III, pp.233–59

Continuation of the Croyland Chronicle, Ingulph's Chronicles, ed. Riley, H. T., London, 1893, pp.501–5

The Rose of England, The English and Scottish Popular Ballads, ed. Child, F. J., 5 vols, New York, 1957, III, pp.331-3

The Song of Lady Bessy, Bishop Percy's Folio Manuscript. Ballads and Romances, ed. Hales, J. W. and Furnivall, F. J., 3 vols, London, 1868, III, pp.319–63

The battlefield memorial, with the royal banner fluttering nearby, stands to the north-west of Ambion Hill, and was put up to mark the spot where Richard fell. This was based on the supposition that the Stanleys were to the north of the field rather than to the south, and that he actually died at Sandeford, where a road for carts from sandpits crossed a stream. Many now dispute both the Stanley positions and the site of Richard's death; moreover, the paucity of information about the battle negates any attempt to mark the site of Richard's death so precisely. It remains, however, a poignant monument to a brave man.

Stoke Golding is marked by the post-medieval spire of the church of St Margaret with Crown Hill to the right. The first reference to this name appears in 1605, the place traditionally associated with the crowning of Henry Tudor. In 1622 William Burton recounts finds of weapons around the lordship of Stoke; in the late 18th century John Nichols mentions many skeletons being dug up during gravel extractions for road repairs.

WARGAMING BOSWORTH

In writing these notes, it has been assumed that the wargamer wishing to re-create the campaign which ended on the field of Bosworth will be using traditional wargame figures on a playing surface. Such aspects as committee games and role playing have not been considered.

Events Leading to the Battle

Without wishing to duplicate the author's excellent text, it is useful to briefly consider those events prior to the battle which can have an interesting bearing on the war game and which are important aspects for the wargamer wishing to peer behind the action itself.

That said, there is absolutely nothing to prevent the wargamer simply deploying the forces (more of which anon) and 'getting stuck in' to the battle itself, without any reference to the build up.

Indeed, one could reasonably argue that re-enacting the campaign proves nothing, for if wargame events do not follow the historical ones, then the battle of Bosworth might well not take place, which would be rather self-defeating.

Fair comment, but the landing of Henry Tudor in Pembrokeshire, the subsequent taking of Dale Castle and Henry's army increasing in strength as he marched across Wales and England are intriguing possibilities.

The English Channel seems to have been enjoying a spell of good weather and the sea was calm as Henry's fleet made the voyage from Harfleur to the Pembroke-shire coast. But what if the weather worsened in mid-Channel, scattering the fleet – as had happened on a previous invasion attempt by Henry – and forcing the individual captains to seek refuge or perhaps landfall where they could. Would the scattered elements of Henry's army be able to re-form, or would those that did make landfall be defeated piecemeal by King Richard's troops?

We are not told much about Dale Castle, but it seems to have been taken fairly easily. Suppose it held out, forcing Henry into a perhaps minor siege that he neither wanted nor was equipped for?

The church of St James the Greater of Dadlington. The late 18th-century antiquary John Nichols records a number of bones being dug up in the vicinity of the church and village.

Finally, what if the contingents that joined the two armies at various points did not do so, or joined with half or double the actual historical numbers?

These are all intriguing points which the campaign war gamer might wish to consider.

Henry Tudor's (Lancastrian) Army

As ever with medieval battles, precise details on the strengths of the opposing armies are difficult to ascertain. Estimates always vary widely as doubtless the writers of accounts were seeking to exult their heroes or masters, while reducing the achievements of the enemy, or those now fallen from favour, at one and the same time.

The present author has arrived at a figure, however, and it is fitting to follow his research on this point.

Henry deployed most of his 5,000 strong army in just one large division under the Earl of Oxford, an experienced commander.

This body of men must have included Welsh archers, French and Scottish mercenaries, with English infantry stationed on the flanks. A small body of mounted knights – including Henry himself – brought up the rear.

Richard III's (Yorkist) Army

It appears that the Yorkist army may well have deployed into three 'battles' or divisions and total around 8,000 men. Such a deployment cannot be proved, but it was in keeping with the military thinking of the day and in purely war game terms, provides an attractive counterpoint to the mass of the Lancastrians.

Using other references in order to arrive at numbers more helpful to a war game re-creation of the battle, it might be assumed that Duke of Norfolk commanded the vanguard of 1,200 archers, flanked with 200 heavily armoured knights under his son Lord Surrey.

The king with the main battle had 1,000 billmen and 2,000 pikemen, while the Earl of Northumberland commanded the rearguard of 2,000 billmen with 1,500 horsemen on the flanks.

One really difficult point is the questionable presence of artillery in the Yorkist army. There are half references to artillery, but details are very imprecise, but it does seem likely that some guns were present with the Yorkist forces at Bosworth.

The wargamer is free to adopt, change or reject these totals, they are merely presented as one set of ideas to assist the wargamer in re-creating the Yorkist army at Bosworth.

Overall, this probably contentious breakdown provides an army of almost 8,000 men.

The Stanley Forces

To the north of the two armies on Ambion Hill, was a third and very large body of troops under Lord Thomas Stanley (2,000–3,000) – who was Henry Tudor's stepfather – and Sir William Stanley (3,000), who had promised Henry support but were not as yet willing to commit themselves since King Richard, suspecting treachery, was holding Lord Strange, Lord Stanley's son, as a hostage against Stanley 'as insurance'.

The early 16th-century brass of Sir William Catesby, at Ashby St Legers, Northamptonshire. Catesby was captured two days after the battle and executed at Leicester.

The Stanleys thus commanded a not inconsiderable and uncommitted force of 5,000–6,000 men.

Figure Scale

Given actual historical armies of 5,000 and 8,000 men, the wargamer has to decide what man/figure ratio to adopt for the re-fight. Much will depend on the figure resource and playing area available, but the following tabulated man/figure ratios will perhaps provide a ready picture:

Size 5,000

At 1:200	1:150	1:100	1:50	1:25	1:10
25 figs	37 figs	50 figs	100 figs	200 figs	500 figs

Army size 8,000

At 1:200	1:150	1:100	1:50	1:25	1:10
40 figs	53 figs	80 figs	160 figs	320 figs	800 figs

Once the man/figure ratio which best suits figure availability, playing area and appearance has been selected, the two armies can be further sub-divided pro rata into the various divisions or troop types.

Taking the 1:25 ratio as an example:

The Lancastrian Army

We simply do not know precise breakdown of troop types in the 5,000 strong Lancastrian army, but the 200 figures are deployed mainly in one large division. This division includes 80 French mercenaries (2,000 came over with Henry) and a lesser number of Scottish mercenaries – another 35 figures – with the rest of the division consisting of 55 figures of Welsh archers. English infantry was stationed on the flanks. There would not be too many of these, so allow say two groups each of 12 figures, being mainly the retinues of the nobles riding with Henry Tudor. The small body of mounted knights – including Henry himself – bringing up the rear could be depicted by no more than six mounted figures. Total: 200 figures.

The Yorkist Army

Following the breakdown above, Richard's 8,000 strong army could be represented as follows:

Vanguard: 48 archer figures, flanked with 12 heavily armoured knights.
Main battle: 40 billmen and 80 pikemen.
Rearguard: 80 billmen with 60 horsemen.
Total: 320 figures

Given a 1:25 ratio, artillery should not really appear on the Bosworth war game table, as it is unlikely that Richard had 25 pieces of artillery. However, for the sake of appearance, perhaps one cannon could be permitted.

The Stanley Forces

140 figures under Lord Thomas Stanley
60 figures under Sir William Stanley

The plaque near Bow Bridge in Leicester commemorating the burial place of Richard III. First placed on view in the Newarke, the body was buried in Grey Friars but this was pulled down during the Reformation and the remains thrown in the River Soar.

It is not at all clear as to just what troop types the Stanleys commanded. As a very rough guide, one might duplicate the Yorkist army in type and possibly organisation.

Total: 200 figures.

It must be stressed that the quoted troop types and strengths, along with the outlined man/figure ratios, are no more than suggestions, leaving the wargamer free to adopt, amend or reject them as required.

Terrain

From Sutton Cheney Ambion Hill spreads westwards before sloping down to a level area across which flowed the Sence Brook.

At the foot of the slope of Ambion Hill was a large area of marshy ground, although, as we have learned from the text, the precise location of this feature is difficult to determine today. For war gaming purposes, it is surely sufficient to follow the author's reasoning that the marsh was sited about 300-400 metres from Ambion Hill

Both Ambion Hill and the marsh are important terrain features and would need to be represented on the war games table. The flat-topped hill is around 400 feet high and needs to be represented by two, possibly three contours placed relatively closely together to provide a fairly steep slope.

A death mask of Henry Tudor. Above the eye can be seen the clotting of the grease used in making the mould. The nose was missing for a long time and the difficult task of reinstating it has resulted in making it rather too bulbous and broad at the tip. (By permission of the Dean and Chapter of Westminster)

The marsh area can be represented in a number of ways, by a piece of felt or similar material, or by a length of cotton or string marking the perimeter, or by a scattering of isolated, small clumps of lichen. The marsh should form an imprecise triangle shape, with its base covering the area at the foot of the southern slope of Ambion Hill and its apex pointing away from the hill. One is tempted to suggest that as a rough rule of thumb, the marsh should have an area which approximates to half that of the hill.

The hill slopes will severely limit movement both upwards and downwards and the marsh acts as an impassable barrier.

Other than these two features, the addition of a few trees, the odd building or two and some decorative lichen will finish off the terrain for Bosworth.

Deployment

Richard's army was drawn up on Ambion Hill in three divisions in column. The vanguard under the Duke of Norfolk was, as one might expect, positioned at the front, followed by the main body and the rearguard behind these two formations.

Henry's army was deployed in one main body, probably behind a 'forward' of archers. As this body advanced towards the Yorkist position, their right was protected by the marsh. Henry himself was positioned to the left rear of his main body with a small body of mounted men-at-arms.

Norfolk moved his men down the south-western slopes of Ambion Hill to engage Henry's men led by the Earl of Oxford. Norfolk was reinforced by more men from the main body under Sir Robert Brackenbury.

It is not quite clear where the Stanleys were deployed – indeed it is a fascinating question to explore – the north-west of the main battlefield will suffice for the wargame, though the south-east seems just as likely.

The Battle

Following an exchange of arrows, the rival armies closed in for a general mêlée, with Norfolk leading his men against Henry's men under Oxford.

Henry's men fought well and held their position. King Richard led an attack by his close companions and some 800 mounted men on Henry Tudor, cutting down William Brandon, his standard-bearer, but was himself killed shortly afterwards. At this point Sir William Stanley fell on the Yorkist flank and Richard's army fled.

The battle was a decisive Lancastrian victory, following which Henry Tudor, Earl of Richmond, was crowned Henry VII. Henry married Elizabeth, daughter of Edward IV, thus ending the dynastic quarrel and the Wars of the Roses, although there was to be one final battle two years later at Stoke Field before the fighting was finally over.

The Mechanics of the Bosworth War Game

Despite the relatively small numbers involved, Bosworth was one of the most important battles in English history, restoring stability and establishing the strong central administration of the Tudor dynasty.

There are a number of points to consider when re-creating Bosworth on the wargame table.

Figure Size

Given two armies of 5,000 and 8,000 men, it would seem that 15mm figures are perhaps the very best size for re-fighting the battle. The 15mm figure permits the wargamer to field reasonable forces and yet permits a manageable playing area – certainly one could comfortably fight Bosworth on an eight feet by five feet wargames table using 15mm figures.

Moving up a size, the use of 25mm figures provides a more spectacular scene, but requires a much larger playing area, although 20mm figures could well be used without too much trouble. Individually based 25mm figures are absolutely ideal for medieval warfare as the opposing troops inevitably become hopelessly intermingled during mêlée.

The use of 6mm figures would mean that the battle

After his crowning, Henry fulfilled his pledge to marry Edward IV's daughter, Elizabeth of York. This gilt bronze effigy was cast by Pietro Torrigiano between about 1512 and 1519. (By permission of the Dean and Chapter of Westminster)

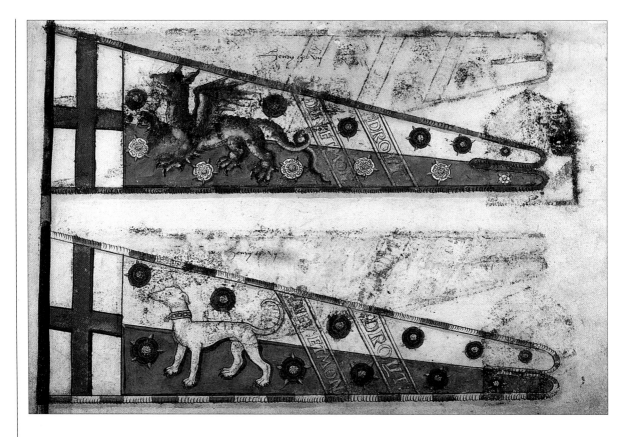

Early 16th-century illustrations of two standards of Henry VII, with his badges of a dragon and a greyhound. (College of Arms, MS. I. 2, p.26)

could be fought on terrain measuring four feet by two feet, but the wargamer would probably lose the sense of the ebbing and flowing of a medieval mêlée.

Commanders

Some wargamers like to reflect their assessment of the various commanders in table-top actions.

Richard III was a sound, reliable commander and a courageous fighter who had served his brother loyally under arms in the north against the Scots. He had also fought at Barnet and Tewkesbury. Against this, he was a cold creature who kept his own counsel and went his own way; he made some awful blunders – such as executing Lord Hastings – and when he most needed friends he found that their 'friendship' was but a veneer covering hatred and suspicion.

The Duke of Norfolk and the Earl of Northumberland were both loyal and competent commanders.

Henry was courageous if inexperienced. Although no warrior endowed with personal valour, he had sufficient of the adventurer and gambler in his make-up to take chances.

The Earl of Oxford was an experienced and important commander who, to all intents and purposes, did Henry's fighting for him at Bosworth.

Lord Stanley was an inexperienced and distrusted commander.

How these characteristics are interpreted for the purposes of Bosworth war game is largely up to the individual wargamer, but there seems little case for radically re-grading – be it up or down – any of the main commanders.

Rules

Any set of late medieval period rules should suffice for this wargame. The customary initial exchange of archery fire – at Bosworth the longbows so often fired at the French were turned on one another – the fierce and bloody infantry mêlée, the cavalry attack are all standard medieval tactics. Only the use of artillery, to whatever degree, will push Bosworth into the later period.

There are also some rule sets specifically designed for the Wars of the Roses period and these would be a useful starting point. One note of caution, the war gamer probably could not realistically use the De Bellis Multitudinis 3000BC to AD1500 rules produced by Wargames Research Group as they are too generalised for re-creating a specific battle.

POINTS TO CONSIDER

Following the Historical Pattern

When re-fighting a particular battle, it is important to adhere as closely as possible to the original historical engagement. The counter argument is that the wargamer(s) know who is going to win. Fair comment perhaps, but knowing the outcome of any battle does not usually prevent one from reading about that action, so why should such knowledge debar a re-fight?

The forces, the terrain and the deployment at least should all be as close to the original set-up as is possible within the wargamer's resources. Additionally, at least the initial moves of the respective commanders need to be re-created. Unless this happens, then an interesting medieval battle may well take place, but it will not be a re-creation of Bosworth.

How many Players?

Unusually in a wargame, the re-fight of Bosworth lends itself to a three-player set-up. Henry, Richard and Lord Stanley are the main three, but one could add the Earl of Oxford and the Duke of Northumberland to this list, perhaps for a club project to involve more players.

Variables

Given the earlier remarks regarding historical accuracy, war gamers are notorious for fiddling with history. Bosworth can offer a number of possibilities in this area.

In addition to the suggested campaign variations, the biggest 'variable' must be the Stanleys. What happens if (a) they go to the aid of the Yorkists, not the Lancastrians; (b) the two brothers argue and each supports one of the two factions; (c) they remain uninvolved?

The presence of French and Scottish mercenaries in Henry's army must give rise to possibilities of changing sides or simply leaving – particularly the French, who seem to have been the product of French jails.

Some variables then, but to repeat the earlier caution – any diversion from the historical may be interesting, but it is not a re-fight of Bosworth.

INDEX

GLOSSARY

ahlspiess a weapon, a square spike on a shaft (p21)

armet a type of helmet (pp18,20)

ballock dagger dagger with two small swellings at base of grip (p21)

barbut type of helmet (pp18, 25, 29, 36)

bard horse armour (p20)

besagew a circular piece of armour to protect the armpit (pp18,25)

bevor defence for the lower face (p18)

bill weapon like an agricultural billhook (p21)

bodkin type of arrowhead (pp22, 37)

bombard heavy siege artillery piece (p23)

brigantine canvas jacket lined with iron plates (pp20, 28)

buckler small, round shield (p20)

cog type of ship (p35)

commissions of array conscription visits to towns and shires (p16)

couter armour to protect the elbow (pp18, 25)

culet armour protecting the buttocks (p22)

falchion weapon like a cleaver (p21)

fauld armour defending the hip (pp18, 25)

glaive weapon combining a blade and a spike (p21)

goat's foot lever device for drawing a crossbow (p22)

hackbut type of handgun (p23)

halberd weapon combining and axe and a spike (pp21,32)

indenture contract cut in two along a wavy line, each party keeping half (p16)

jack quilted protective jacket, sometimes sleeveless (p20)

kettle hat a type of helmet (p28)

livery and maintenance a privilege conferred on reliable nobles permitting them to keep private armies (p16)

mail armour formed of interlinked metal rings

match a fuse for igniting gunpowder (p22)

maul a mallet for driving stakes into the ground (p21)

pavise a shield used by crossbowmen (p22)

plackart armour defending the stomach (p18)

points waxed laces to secure armour (p18)

poleyn armour protecting the knee (pp18, 25)

pollaxe weapon comprising spear, axe and hammer (pp21, 33)

pursuivant lowest class of heraldic officer, below a herald

ravensbill a pollaxe

retainers followers of a lord (p16)

rondel dagger dagger with a disc each end of the grip (p21)

sabaton armour defending the foot (p18)

sallet type of helmet (pp18, 27)

scurriers foragers, food-hunters (p17)

scutage money paid instead of doing military service (p17)

serpentine light artillery piece (pp23, 50)

skull-cap rimless helmet (p20)

slow-match a fuse for igniting gunpowder (p22)

splint a form of armour (p19)

tabard garment worn over armour (p19)

tassets armour plates hanging from the hip defence, the fauld (pp18, 25)

war hammer a one-handed weapon (p75)

PLACES TO VISIT

Central England

The Battle of Bosworth, Bosworth Battlefield Visitor Centre, Sutton Cheney, near Market Bosworth, eight miles west of Leicester by A47, B582, B585 and A447. Open April to October daily 1pm to 6pm; July and August opens at 11am. See page 83.

The Battle of Stoke Field, 16 June 1487. East Stoke, 3 miles south-west of Newark-on-Trent by A46, and west by minor road, Church Lane.

A Yorkist group commanded by the Earl of Lincoln had Lambert Simnel crowned as Edward VI in Dublin in May 1487 and landed in Lancashire with 2,000 Swiss and German mercenaries under Martin Schwartz and 4,000 Irish troops. They made for York which they failed to take, but forced Henry VII's followers to stay there as they turned south with their numbers grown to some 8,000 men. Henry met George Stanley, Lord Strange, near Nottingham and moved to meet Lincoln. The Yorkists crossed the Trent at Fiskerton, by a ford now long gone, and took position on a ridge. From Church Lane off the A46 towards St Oswald's church, Humber Lane runs to the left towards the ridge and from Church Lane after it turns left beyond the church a footpath goes to the western end of the high ground, with a view to the river crossing to the north west. Trent Lane, a track opposite Lodge Lane, off the A46 south of East Stoke, is roughly the position reached by Henry's army.

The Earl of Oxford, leading the royal vanguard, was coming up the Fosse Way (now A46) when he saw the Yorkist force off to his left. He hurried his men to face them and Lincoln seized the opportunity to attack. Oxford's men were pushed back and suffered high casualties, but the rest of Henry's army eventually came up and the balance swung in their favour. In the centre the Swiss and German soldiers fought on doggedly, but the rest of the Yorkist force turned tail, pursued by the victors. As they made back to the river they were cut down in such numbers, 4,000 died, that the gully that runs through the wood is now called the Red Gutter.

The Battle of Tewkesbury, 4 May 1471. Marked trail south of the town.

Edward IV overcame the Lancastrian army at Barnet on 14 April 1471, the day Queen Margaret and the Prince of Wales landed at Weymouth to restore the captured Henry VI to the throne. Margaret made for the Severn in the hope of gaining Welsh support and of moving north to gather further strength in Cheshire. Edward marched from Windsor to cut her off, but was tricked into expecting to fight at Sodbury Hill, halfway between Bristol and Malmesbury. The Lancastrians gave him the slip and marched on to Berkeley, making for the Severn crossing at Gloucester, but Edward's messenger arrived there first and by 10am on 3 May she found the town closed against her. Meanwhile Edward was pushing north along the hilltop edge towards Cheltenham. Margaret made for the next crossing at Tewkesbury, arriving there with some 5,000 exhausted troops that afternoon and Edward's force of about 3,000 made it to Tredington that evening.

The Gloucester Road at Tewkesbury at that time ran approximately along the line of the footpath south from the A38 opposite the cemetery, which is part of the battle trail. The Cheltenham road was to the east of the modern road, nearer Swilgate Brook. A low ridge runs at right angles to these across the approach to the town, and this was where the Lancastrians formed up with the Prince of Wales in nominal command of the centre, actually under Lord Wenlock, the Earl of Devonshire on their left and the commander-in-chief, the Duke of Somerset, on the right. Edward was in the centre of his line with his brother, Richard of Gloucester, on his left and Hastings on the right. It seems likely that the left covered the old Gloucester road, the right the old

Cheltenham road, and Edward was thus on the ridge along which the modern road runs. Fearing attack from the wooded hill known as the Park, south-west of the town and flanking his position, Edward sent 200 spearmen to check it and, if they found it clear, to await developments.

Somerset planned a double stroke with an attack on Edward's left coupled with a frontal assault by Wenlock on the centre. However, when he fell on Gloucester's men the spearmen from the Park took his men in the flank while Wenlock stood still. The Lancastrian right was pushed back and put to the sword in Bloody Meadow along Coln Brook and the banks of the Avon. Somerset, it is said, infuriated by the apparent treachery, rode up to Wenlock and smashed his head in. The Lancastrian army fell apart and the Prince of Wales was killed; ending the Lancastrian line.

Fotheringhay Castle Fotheringhay, 7 miles east of Peterborough by A605 and minor road. Open site.

Of a castle with two outstanding historical associations there remains only a series of grassy mounds. Here Richard III was born and here Mary, Queen of Scots, was executed.

A Norman motte and bailey was built overlooking the crossing of the River Nene in the 12th century and the remains of the motte still stand here. The original moat was filled in when the inner bailey was extended in the 14th century and the keep rebuilt in stone. The new bailey was protected on the south-west by the river from which a moat was cut, starting some 150 yards from the modern bridge and curving anti-clockwise within the space between the river and the modern farm track. The great hall stood in the south-eastern corner. At much the same time an outer bailey was added, with a moat running from the modern bridge to the right of the road into the village, and then turning right north-east of the farm track and broadening into a lake before turning back to the river by joining the mill stream. Much of this can be worked out on the ground.

North-west of the castle stands the curiously proportioned parish church. It is all that remains of the buildings of the College of St Mary and All Saints which was a Chantry college. With the help of the booklet on sale within, a visit is rewarding and stained glass windows commemorate Richard III.

Northern England

The Battle of Towton, 29 March 1461. Towton, 10 miles south-west of York by A64, A162 and B1217 to Battlefield Cross (viewpoint).

The Wars of the Roses were finely balanced in early 1461. The Lancastrians had won a close contest at the Second Battle of St Albans, but were too weak to attempt to take London and retired north. Meanwhile Edward IV had gained a clear victory at Mortimer's Cross and, having had himself proclaimed king in London, was determined to make his position secure. He gathered his forces and set off to Pontefract and thence to Ferrybridge where, on Saturday, 28 March, a fierce engagement took place in which Lord Clifford prevented the Yorkist Lord Fauconberg from crossing the River Aire. Edward sent Faunconberg in again to cross the river higher up successfully, and Clifford was caught and killed at Dintingdale.

Palm Sunday dawned in snow and wind. The Lancastrians, under the Duke of Somerset, had taken up position south of Towton with their right near the Battlefield Cross, the flank protected by the deep valley of the River Cock, and the left on the Ferrybridge road (A162). South of the valley they faced is another ridge, with Castle Hill Wood standing above the river and the village of Saxton south of it. The Yorkists occupied this ridge with their left just north of the junction with the lane to Saxton and their right straddling the Ferrybridge road, the wind at their backs blowing the snow into the faces of their enemies. The Yorkists advanced briefly to loose a volley of arrows and as swiftly retired, allowing the answering fire to fall short. A Lancastrian advance was assisted by a flanking force concealed in Castle Hill Wood, but the two sides locked together in a long, murderous mass. For three hours the slaughter continued. At last the Duke of Norfolk's men came up from Ferrybridge to turn the Lancastrian left flank and force Somerset's men back towards the river over which they attempted to flee to York by way of Tadcaster. The Yorkist cavalry pursued and cut them down. Some 20,000 Lancastrians died and about 8,000 Yorkists lost their lives – the costliest battle on English soil.

The Battle of Wakefield, 30 December 1460 Sandal Castle, off the A61 south of Wakefield, nine miles south of Leeds by A61.
With the defeat of the Royal army at Northampton in July, the Duke of York was able to obtain an Act of Settlement that declared him and his issue heirs to Henry VI. Queen Margaret reacted at once to the exclusion of her son, Edward, from the throne and gathered the Lancastrian forces in the north. York hastened from London to his castle of Sandal, two miles south of Wakefield and at the time in a landscape of field and forest. The Yorkists were outnumbered by the Lancastrian army, which may have had as many as 12,000 men, and doubtless welcomed the proposal of a truce over Christmas. The reinforcements so gladly received at Sandal were actually enemy infiltrators, and when Sir Andrew Trollope turned up on 30 December with more men near the bend in the River Calder north-west of the castle, York may well have thought them further troops coming to aid him. In any case, he unwisely sallied forth from the security of the castle to find himself beset not only by the new arrivals he could see, but also by additional Lancastrian soldiers hidden in the woods to the north-east and south-west. More than 2,000 Yorkists fell, including York himself and his younger son Edmund.

Middleham Castle, Middleham, 12 miles south-west of Richmond, Yorkshire, by A6108. English Heritage. Tel: (01969) 623899.
Shop. Open April to October 10am to 6pm, November to March Wednesday to Sunday 10am to 1pm and 2pm to 4pm.
In the 1170s Robert fitzRalph started the work on the construction of a great rectangular stone keep on two floors. In the 14th century the whole was heightened and a new window added as outer defences lessened the military role of the keep. The remaining outer walls are those of the 14th century. Middleham was a centre of power in the north under the Nevilles who held it from the late 13th century until 1471, when Richard, Earl of Warwick, the Kingmaker, was killed at Barnet and the castle was forfeit to the Crown. Edward IV gave it to his brother who was to become Richard III.

The Royal Armouries, The Waterfront, Leeds. Tel: (0990) 106666 or (0113) 245 6456. Open April to August 10am to 5pm, 6pm at weekends and in school holidays; September to March until 4pm, 5pm weekends.
The collection of the Royal Armouries, the exhibition of which was formerly limited to what could be shown at the Tower of London, is now the basis of a museum that makes use of the most modern techniques of presentation. Three thousand years of warfare can be experienced here and it has the finest collection of medieval arms and armour in Britain. The global development of arms and armour is presented using film, computer interactive technology, object handling sessions and live demonstrations.

Southern England

The Battle of Barnet, 14 April 1471 Monken Hadley, north of Barnet, on A1000, or two miles south-west of Potter's Bar from junction 24, M25. Underground station: High Barnet.

Richard Neville, Earl of Warwick, the Kingmaker, switched his loyalty to the Lancastrians and restored Henry VI to the throne in 1470 forcing Edward IV to flee to Burgundy on 2 October. Edward was back the next spring with a force supported by Charles the Bold and bottled Warwick up at Coventry before regaining London on 12 April. Warwick had brought the Lancastrian army south but Edward had quickly consolidated and was at Barnet to push back the Lancastrian advance guard on the night of 13 April. The Yorkists camped that night astride the Great North Road north of the junction with St Albans Road with Edward in the centre, Lord Hastings to the west on St Albans Road and Richard of Gloucester far to the east on Hadley Wood Road. The Lancastrians were on the north of Hadley Green on a line through the golf clubhouse on the west and north of Dury Road and the church to the east, with the Duke of Somerset in the centre, the Earl of Oxford on the west and Warwick himself on the east.

Early in the morning Edward's troops advanced through the mist. The Yorkist line was overlapped on the west by Oxford but out-flanked Warwick in the east. Thus, when they met, Oxford was able to push Hastings's men back though Barnet, but there the victors dispersed, either to loot the village or chase the fleeing Yorkists. On the other flank Warwick was hard pressed by Gloucester, but was holding on as the centre locked together in battle. Oxford managed to get his troops together again and they returned to the battlefield but, as they were coming from the south, their Lancastrian fellows assumed they had changed sides and fired upon them as freely as they did on the Yorkists. At this moment Edward threw his reserves into the fight and the Lancastrians broke. Warwick never reached his horse in the rear of his position, he was caught and killed. That evening Queen Margaret landed at Weymouth to reinforce the Lancastrian cause. Lacking Warwick, she was to see it destroyed at Tewkesbury three weeks later.

The Tower of London, Tower Hill, London. Tel: (020) 7600 3699. Open March to October Monday to Saturday 9am to 6pm, Sunday 10am to 5pm. November to February the same, but closes 5pm. Underground station: Tower Hill.
Here Bishop Gandulf of Rochester built William the Conqueror a stone keep, later called the White Tower. The additional defences to be seen today were started by Richard I and Edward I started the outer ring of defence, completed by Edward III, which included a water-gate, St Thomas's Tower, popularly known as the Traitor's Gate. Here Richard III probably imprisoned the unfortunate princes, though no one is sure where they were actually kept.

The Royal Armouries are in the White Tower. Open March to October Sunday 10am to 5pm, Monday to Saturday 9am to 5pm. Closes 4pm November to February.
The bulk of the collection having been relocated in Leeds, the new displays here tell the story of the building and development of the White Tower and of the Royal Armoury itself, and of the Board of Ordnance which was responsible for the development of new weapons until 1855. The personal armours of Tudor and Stuart royalty are here.

RICHARD III SOCIETY
4 Oakley Street, Chelsea, London SW3 5NN. Website: www.r3.org

TRAVELLER'S REFERENCES
Marix Evans, Martin, *The Military Heritage of Britain and Ireland* André Deutsch, 1998.
Seymour, William, *Battles in Britain*, Wordsworth, 1997.
Smurthwaite, David, *The Complete Guide to the Battlefields of Britain* Michael Joseph, 1993.